BEAR WITH ME

BEAR WITH ME

*A Family History of George Halas
and the Chicago Bears*

Patrick McCaskey
with Mike Sandrolini

TRIUMPH
BOOKS

Library of Congress Cataloging-in-Publication Data

McCaskey, Patrick, 1949–
  Bear with me : a family history of George Halas and the Chicago Bears / Patrick McCaskey, with Mike Sandrolini.
    p. cm.
  ISBN 978-1-60078-128-5
  1. Halas, George, 1895–1983. 2. Chicago Bears (Football team) 3. Sports team owners—United States—Biography. I. Sandrolini, Mike. II. Title.
  GV939.H26M44 2009
  796.332092—dc22
  [B]
                                                                    2009010158

This book is available in quantity at special discounts for your group or organization. For further information, contact:

Triumph Books
542 South Dearborn Street
Suite 750
Chicago, Illinois 60605
(312) 939-3330
Fax (312) 663-3557
www.triumphbooks.com

Printed in U.S.A.
ISBN: 978-1-60078-128-5
Design by Patricia Frey
Photos courtesy of Patrick McCaskey and the Chicago Bears unless otherwise indicated

This book is dedicated to my grandfather, George Halas; my grandmother, Min Halas; my uncle, Mugs Halas; my aunt, Pat Halas; my father, Ed McCaskey; and my mother, Virginia McCaskey. They are listed in alphabetical order. This book is a thank-you note to them.

"Nobody who ever gave his best regretted it."

—*George Halas*

CONTENTS

INTRODUCTION

I happened to be working as a sportswriter for my hometown newspaper, the *Daily News-Tribune* in LaSalle, Illinois, during the mid-1980s—an era during which the Bears were one of the NFL's most dominant teams. One blistering hot summer day in late July 1985, I decided to hop into my three-speed, stick shift Dodge Omni and make the trek to Platteville, Wisconsin—the community that played host to the Bears' summer training camp—in order to get a firsthand look at "Iron Mike" Ditka's squad.

There they were, all the personalities that made those teams so special—Walter Payton, Dan Hampton, Steve "Mongo" McMichael, "Samurai" Mike Singletary, the punky QB known as McMahon, "Mama's Boy" Otis Wilson, Willie Gault, "L.A." Mike Richardson, and the rookie, William "the Refrigerator" Perry.

The sight of the Fridge sitting in an ice tub after practice wearing nothing but a pair of gym shorts is still etched in my mind to this day.

However, another man made quite an impression on me that afternoon, for all the right reasons: Mike McCaskey, who was then the Bears' president.

I remember standing a few feet away from Mike at one point during the afternoon practice session. I pulled out my tape recorder, introduced myself, and started asking him questions about the team. He greeted me warmly and answered every query. It was like having a conversation with my next-door neighbor.

I'm sure Mike's younger brother, Patrick—the team's director of community involvement and travel manager at the time—was somewhere around the field that day. But I wouldn't meet Pat for another decade. When we did meet, Pat also would have to face my tape recorder as I was given the assignment of interviewing him for a magazine article. The story centered around Pat's duties with the Bears and his Christian faith.

During our discussion, Pat explained—thoughtfully and in soft tones like his brother—that the Chicago Bears are more than the NFL's hallmark franchise. It's a family. It doesn't matter if you happen to be a Halas, a McCaskey, a player, a coach, a team employee, or a fan. You are part of the Bears' family.

One of George S. Halas' 13 grandchildren, Pat has been an integral part of the Bears organization for more than 35 years, and he's been around the team all his life. So it should come as no surprise that family is a recurring theme throughout this book.

It's taken Pat years to compile and compose all the stories you'll find inside. He provides great detail on the life and times of his grandfather, George Halas—how he grew up in Chicago; became a three-sport athlete at the University of Illinois; took a job at A.E. Staley Company in Decatur to become player/coach of the company's football team; got the green light to move the team from Decatur to Chicago; changed its name from the Staleys to the Bears; made them a charter member of the new American Professional Football Association (which later became the NFL), then led them through great years and lean years, through the Great Depression and a world war, through the 1963 NFL championship, and into the era of Gale Sayers and Dick Butkus.

But Pat also expounds on George Halas, the man, by giving insight on how Papa Bear influenced Pat's life, and how he loved and cared for his family, his friends, and those who played for him.

In addition, Pat will tell you all about what it was like growing up in the Edward and Virginia McCaskey household with his seven brothers and three sisters.

Woven in with these stories are interesting accounts and tidbits on great Bears teams, players, and personalities.

It's been an honor and privilege to help Pat put this book together. I trust you'll enjoy it.

—Mike Sandrolini

Chapter 1

MISSING THE BOAT

My grandfather, George Stanley Halas—founder of the Chicago Bears and the National Football League—was born on February 2, 1895, to Barbara and Frank J. Halas in an apartment on 18th Place and Wood Street in Chicago. He was the youngest of eight children, but of those eight, only four survived infancy: George, his brothers, Walter and Frank, and his sister, Lillian.

Grandpa grew up in a bohemian neighborhood just southwest of downtown Chicago. His father ran a tailoring business, but later suffered a stroke and ended up selling the business. Frank eventually had a three-story building constructed at 18th and Wood, which had an apartment on each floor and a grocery store/dairy shop at ground level that Barbara ran. Unfortunately, his father passed away while Grandpa was attending Crane Tech High School.

At Crane, Grandpa went out for football, track, and baseball, but struggles with his weight—specifically, an inability to gain any—turned out to be an issue. Grandpa weighed 110 pounds when he started at Crane, yet despite eating everything his mother put on the table (and then some), he had managed to put on just 10 more pounds by the time he graduated.

My grandfather (front row, middle) on the Crane Tech baseball team.

Grandpa met his future wife, Min, while pitching for Crane one day against Harrison High School. Min attended the rival school, and she heckled both Grandpa and his catcher during the game. That caught Grandpa's attention, but in a good way. Shortly thereafter, they began seeing each other.

Upon graduating from Crane in 1913, it was assumed that Grandpa would immediately follow in older brother Walter's footsteps: he would enroll at the University of Illinois at Urbana-Champaign, become part of the Tau Kappa Epsilon fraternity, and go out for the freshman football team. But the family had other ideas.

Much to his disappointment, the family decided Grandpa would work for a year before entering college. Walter, in particular, minced no words when he told Grandpa that if he had any hopes of playing football in college, he needed to put on some weight.

Grandpa got a job at Western Electric Company, based in nearby Cicero, working in the payroll department (Min also worked at Western Electric). He played for the payroll department's baseball team, and gained some weight during the year, as well.

In the fall of 1914, Grandpa set out for the University of Illinois with nearly 20 extra pounds on his frame, hoping to impress the freshman coach. He enrolled in civil engineering, and the fraternity got him a job as a waiter. However, Grandpa's freshman season on the gridiron didn't turn out quite as well as he had hoped it would. He ended up being a reserve halfback. Grandpa then turned his attention to baseball in the spring and made the freshman baseball team.

Walter and Grandpa returned to Chicago for the summer, and Grandpa resumed working for Western Electric. On July 24, 1915, Western Electric was holding its annual picnic in Michigan City, Indiana, so like many of the other employees, Grandpa purchased a ticket to cross Lake Michigan on the excursion ship, called the *Eastland*, for the trip to Michigan City.

Fortunately for Grandpa, his brother Frank asked him to step on the scale and check his weight just as he was about to leave the house to get on the *Eastland*. Grandpa checked in at 163 pounds, and the delay ended up saving Grandpa's life. When he got to the dock, he learned that the *Eastland* had capsized. The loss of life was appalling; 812 people died when the *Eastland* went down. It was reported that passengers had all lined up on one side of the vessel along the rail to watch the traffic in the Chicago River. The weight of so many people on one side caused the *Eastland* to turn over.

An alert reporter obtained a passenger list, and the next morning Grandpa's name appeared as one of the fatalities. That night the doorbell rang, and when Grandpa answered it, two of his fraternity brothers, Elmer Strumf and Walter Straub, stood there, thinking they were going to extend their condolences to Grandpa's grieving mother. But they were delighted to find Grandpa alive! Suddenly, the magnitude of Grandpa's good fortune overwhelmed him and he readily agreed to his mother's suggestion that he say a rosary of gratitude before he went to bed. Grandpa was always grateful to Frank for his intervention that day.

By comparison, the remainder of the summer was very tame. The night before he and Walter were going to return to Champaign, the family was assembled at the house waiting for the dinner bell when Frank suggested that Grandpa weigh in one last time. Grandpa stalled Frank until after dinner, hoping that he could pack in a pound or two at the table. He knew that he was heavier than he had been in his life. Grandpa stepped on the scale, and after it stopped quivering, Walter shouted, "178 pounds!" Everyone was thrilled, but no one more than Grandpa.

The next day, Walter and Grandpa took the train to Champaign, and Grandpa settled in for his sophomore year. He couldn't wait to report for football. Since his freshman year, he had added 38 pounds and felt that he was ready.

The University of Illinois had a very good team that season under varsity head coach Bob Zuppke. The Illini's best player was Harold Poague, an All-American halfback. But Poague's presence didn't stop Grandpa, who decided to try out for halfback with the intent of taking Poague's place. Coach Zuppke didn't seem too impressed by Grandpa, however, and for the first eight weeks, Grandpa played halfback on the scrub team. Zuppke hadn't even said a word to him. Then one afternoon, Grandpa was running against the first-string defense; time after time, he was knocked down for no gain. Finally, he caught Coach Zuppke's attention.

"Who is that?" Zuppke screamed.

Someone answered, "Halas."

Zuppke hollered, "Get him out of there or he'll get killed."

That ended Grandpa's career as a halfback. Fortunately, the line coach saved Grandpa by making him an end. But as far as Grandpa was concerned, playing end meant being used in scrimmage every afternoon against the first team. It was tough, discouraging work, but Grandpa was determined to catch the eye of at least one of the coaches.

One afternoon, his fortunes changed. The backups were scrimmaging against the varsity when Poague headed toward Grandpa's end on a sweep. When Grandpa attempted to tackle Poague, the star halfback drove his pistonlike legs right into Grandpa's chest and kept right on going. This happened a second and third time, but things finally went Grandpa's way the fourth time Poague was in his vicinity. Grandpa found himself off-balance as Poague approached him, but as he was falling, he reached out and hit Poague in the chest. Poague went down like a ton of bricks! And from that point on, Grandpa had Poague figured out. Whenever Grandpa tackled Poague, it was always chest high, and Poague always went down. Poague was a fearsome runner and would punish every tackler…except for Grandpa.

Later in the year, however, Grandpa's bad luck returned. The backups were on offense against the first-team defense, and one of the varsity players intercepted a pass and was heading for the goal line. Grandpa ran him down and saved a touchdown, but when he dove, he caught the varsity player's heel right in the mouth. Grandpa suffered a broken jaw—his first broken bone ever—and any hopes he had of moving up to the first team were postponed indefinitely. But there was a silver lining to his injury. At least now Coach Zuppke knew who Grandpa was, and the man they called "the little Dutchman" said, "Next year, Halas, you'll play for me."

Interestingly, Potsy Clark, the team's star quarterback, also broke his jaw, and some enterprising young photographer took Clark and Grandpa's photo as they stood together. The picture was used on a postcard with the caption, "The Order of the Broken Jaw." Since Potsy was the campus star, students bought the postcards by the handful. When they mailed the cards to their families and friends, Grandpa profited by association with Potsy. The big lesson Grandpa learned from this experience was the value of a little publicity—something he would take with him years later while he was trying to establish the Bears. George S. Halas didn't become a household name, but when he went home for Christmas that year, several people asked him about his jaw.

Football season ended without Grandpa playing a single minute on the varsity, but his hopes were high for the 1916 season. Schoolwork and waiting tables took all his time. Then suddenly it was spring, and spring meant baseball.

Walter was the star pitcher for Illinois, and manager George Huff welcomed Grandpa to the team's first practice. That year he played right, center, and left field and batted .350. Final exams came, and Walter and Grandpa each did very well. In June, they headed home for the summer with great expectations. Western Electric had notified Grandpa that his job was once again waiting for him, and so was the company baseball team.

The summer seemed to fly by. Grandpa was playing for the Western Electric baseball team, and he also played for the Logan Squares, a semipro club. Of course, his daytime hours were spent on the job in the payroll department. Meanwhile, the family had settled into its new home on the second floor of a building at 23rd and Washtenaw. Grandpa's mother Barbara had gotten rid of the flat building and had sufficient income from her investments to live modestly, yet comfortably. At 23rd and Washtenaw, the family made the front room into a saloon that Grandpa's mother operated with everyone's help. That summer, most of Grandpa's social activities were confined to an occasional soda with Min or a beer with some of the fellows after they had played a baseball game. By the time evening baseball had concluded, Grandpa was ready for bed because he had to be up early the next morning to work.

When the time came for Grandpa to return to Champaign for his junior year, his mother held a dinner meeting, during the course of which she offered him $30 for September because of "extra expenses the first month." Grandpa tried to tell her that he had plenty of money after his summer at Western Electric, along with the money he had accumulated playing baseball, but she insisted he take it. Like clockwork, her check for $25 arrived the first week of October and every month for the remainder of the school year.

Football practice got under way, and Grandpa, who now checked in at 178 pounds, was installed at right end. He did a pretty fair job until he had the misfortune of breaking his leg. At the time, he did not even know the leg was broken. Neither did Coach Zuppke, who one day was conducting an on-field team meeting and got on Grandpa in front of the other players for not giving 100 percent on the field. Grandpa lost his head. He took off his headgear and threw it in Coach Zuppke's direction. Thank goodness, Grandpa made sure he missed the coach. Although this was an act of insubordination, it did have positive results. After that, Zuppke had a little more respect for Grandpa, whom the team later put in a hospital. X-rays revealed that the leg was indeed broken.

After five days in the hospital, Grandpa pleaded to get back to his classes. The doctor liked Grandpa's academic prowess and released him, complete with crutches and a cast. But rather than go to his American history class, he headed straight for football practice. Grandpa attended practice every day, leaning on his crutches, and watched Zuppke prepare his team for the next game.

Coach Zuppke must have liked Grandpa because Zuppke gave him the job of running the athletic store, which in fact was more of an equipment room where he kept the team's supply of socks, jocks, and shirts. There were no athletic scholarships in those days, so the job in the athletic store was quite a plum. Grandpa's mother was paying his tuition and continued to send him $25 a month to supplement his room and board. The job waiting tables complemented that, so for a college student Grandpa found himself in affluent circumstances.

Grandpa's studies were very demanding that year. It had been his plan to load up on credits his first three and a half years in school so that he would be able to coast and enjoy his final semester. But with his heavy class workload, his cast and crutches, his jobs in the athletic store and as a waiter, Grandpa concluded that he was in over his head. He decided to ease the strain by hiring his first employee—another student—to run the store. Grandpa was getting $300 to run the store, so he paid his employee $150 to run the operation while Grandpa pocketed the remaining $150. This worked out very well for the remainder of his stay at Illinois.

After Grandpa broke his leg, Coach Zuppke paid him an honor that he always treasured. Zuppke noticed that Grandpa was at practice every day, intently watching from the sideline. Late in the season, Illinois was scheduled to meet Big Ten power Minnesota in Minneapolis. On the eve of the team's departure, Grandpa was hobbling along on his crutches when Coach Zuppke came up to him.

Zuppke said, "Halas, tomorrow you will go to Minnesota with us."

Grandpa was too dazed to even answer or thank him, but when the train pulled out the next day, he was on board.

Minnesota had a great team in 1916. The Gophers featured an All-American end, Bert Baston, and George Hauser, who became an All-American tackle the following year. Minnesota was expected to beat Illinois by 50 points, but Grandpa didn't care because he was so happy to just be on the sideline with his teammates. It was a great football game. The Illini outplayed the Gophers, stayed on top the entire contest, and won 14–9. When the final gun sounded, Grandpa was so ecstatic he threw his crutches into the air and celebrated with the team as best he could. The Illinois locker room was joyous and exuberant. It was a great ride home.

Walter and Grandpa went home to Chicago to be with the family for Christmas vacation. When the family got together, Grandpa told his mother that due to his job with the athletic store, he wouldn't have to take her monthly check during the second semester. But his mother wouldn't hear of it. She insisted Grandpa's college education was her responsibility and that she would continue to send checks (which, of course, she did).

Walter and Grandpa returned to Champaign after Christmas and decided that they were going to get right down to studying at the TKE fraternity house. One evening while Grandpa was hitting the books, one of the fraternity brothers walked into Grandpa's room to tell him that he had a visitor. When Grandpa reached the living room, much to his surprise, he found Ralph Jones, the coach of Illinois' varsity basketball team. Jones wasted no time and got right to the point of his visit.

Jones said, "George, I want you at basketball practice tomorrow."

Grandpa replied, "Coach, we have exams in a few days, and you know that I broke my leg."

Jones smiled and said, "I know all about the leg, and I also know that I saw you throw your crutches into the air when we beat Minnesota. You'd better be at the gym tomorrow."

Grandpa only had one answer: "Yes, sir."

The next afternoon, Grandpa reported for basketball, and Coach Jones wasted no time getting him into the lineup. The results, however, were less than spectacular. In his first game, he fouled out in just two and a half minutes. Grandpa's job with the team was to play a position that Coach Jones called "back guard." In effect, he stayed in the backcourt and picked up the opposing players when they approached that area.

Basketball under Ralph Jones was great fun. For one thing, Grandpa found that basketball could be a contact sport, and he relished it. Jones taught Grandpa to play with greater finesse than he had ever played previously. The highlight of the season came in the final game versus Wisconsin. Illinois was leading by one point, but the Badgers made a basket and pulled ahead with only 30 seconds to play. Grandpa was dribbling slowly up court when he saw Jones on the sideline waving a towel frantically. Jones was trying to tell Grandpa to pass the ball, but Grandpa misinterpreted his instructions. Instead, Grandpa took a two-handed shot just after he passed midcourt. It seemed like the ball hung in the air forever, but it ended up going through the hoop as the whistle sounded. Illinois had beaten Wisconsin and were champions of the Big Ten.

After the season was over, the team had a banquet to cap off the year. During the evening, Jones announced that George Halas would be the team's captain the following year. Grandpa had a hunch that the Woods twins, Ralph and Ray, had something to do with him becoming captain. Ralph and Ray were outstanding basketball players in their own right…and they also happened to be TKEs.

Basketball had hardly ended when Coach Huff issued the call for baseball. Walter returned as the Illini's established star pitcher. Grandpa performed well in the outfield the previous year, and there was every reason to believe that he would start there again. Walter and Grandpa were the first players to report. They enjoyed a good year in baseball, as Grandpa again batted around .350. Baseball was by far his best sport and was also his favorite.

After baseball came final exams. Shortly thereafter, Walter graduated, and the Halas brothers headed home in June. Grandpa remembered that after he paid his train fare he still had $178…or one dollar for every pound he had managed to keep on his frame.

Usually, family meetings were held on Sundays, but this time the Halas clan had its special dinner on Walter and Grandpa's first night back in Chicago. Walter was the star attraction, and why not? He had achieved the family dream. Walter had earned the first university degree in the family, and everyone was very proud of him. His mother had tears in her eyes, and sat for most of the evening with her arm on the back of Walter's chair.

Walter was the first university graduate and looked forward to big things. As it turned out, Walter had a wonderful life. He'd been a pitcher and shortstop at Illinois. That summer, he went on to pitch in the Rock Island League. After pitching in the Three I League, he went to Somerset, Kentucky, where he coached the Somerset High School football and baseball teams. Later, he played in Davenport, Iowa, where he met his wife, who taught there. Then Walter coached at Davenport High School in 1919.

In 1920 Walter went to Notre Dame. He was head basketball coach and managed the baseball team. The great Knute Rockne was the head track and football coach, while Walter was his assistant and coached the backfield. That was the entire staff for football at Notre Dame in those days; Knute and Walter were also the team trainers and did all the paperwork.

Walter stayed at Notre Dame for two years, then went to Mount St. Mary's College in Maryland to be the head coach and director of athletics. His next stop was Haverford (Pennsylvania) College, where he again served as head football coach and athletics director. He then went to Drexel University in Philadelphia in 1927 and stayed there until 1941. After that, he spent a year at Maryland under Clark Shaughnessy as the freshman coach. Later, during World War II, Grandpa would ask Walter to come to Chicago to help him and Ralph Brizzolara with the Bears and also with a sporting goods business Grandpa had started.

After their happy and bountiful celebration dinner that night, the Halases dispersed and Grandpa had a few minutes alone with his mother. He told her about the $178 he had saved, but when he offered it to her, she refused to take it. She urged him to open a bank account and told him how much she looked forward to the following year, when he would earn the second college degree in the Halas family. Grandpa's mother was a saint, and the family was fortunate to have her with them for many years.

Western Electric and baseball took up Grandpa's time that entire summer until it was time for him to return to Champaign for his senior year. It was strange not having Walter at school with him. However, Grandpa was a big boy now and capable of returning to Champaign on his own. He was anxious for the football season to begin.

The 1917 football campaign turned out to be a very satisfying year for Grandpa. He felt stronger than he had the previous three seasons.

Zuppke used Grandpa on kickoff and punt returns because of his speed. At one point during a game against Wisconsin, Zuppke had Grandpa back for the kickoff...and something strange happened. As the ball floated down to him, it deflated, and when he caught it, little, if any, air remained in it. This caused great consternation, and players on both teams stood around and discussed the matter with the officials.

Finally, it was decided that the proper thing to do was to have Wisconsin kick again with another ball. But Grandpa ended up kicking himself afterward because all he would have had to do was take off and run for the goal line; he would have scored a touchdown during the confusion. He plainly missed the opportunity and always remembered that flat ball in his hands.

At the season-ending football banquet, Coach Zuppke said something that stayed with Grandpa throughout the years. Zuppke said, "Just when I teach you fellows how to play, you graduate and I lose you." That statement became very important to Grandpa a few years later.

Basketball followed almost immediately, and Grandpa was looking forward to the season as the team's new captain. At the end of the first semester of his senior year (or midway through the basketball season), he needed only six credit hours to graduate. He intended to have the fun that he never had time for prior to his senior year.

The only problem was that the United States had entered World War I.

Chapter 2

IN THE NAVY

The United States entered World War I in April 1917, and the country had little time for anything else. The newspapers were full of stories about our armed forces. Grandpa felt that it was his duty to enlist, but his mother kept pleading with him to get his degree before doing so. On campus, Illinois had an ROTC unit, which prepared young college men for active service. Grandpa had never been able to take ROTC because it conflicted with athletics.

At the time, the ROTC unit was under the command of a regular army officer, Major Edward W. McCaskey. He was very tough about not missing ROTC drills, so it was practically impossible for athletes to be members of his unit. (At the time, McCaskey's name didn't mean much to Grandpa, but he certainly remembered it many years later when his daughter Virginia married McCaskey's grandson and namesake.)

Grandpa's mother was adamant about her son receiving his degree, but he wanted to serve his country. Since Grandpa much preferred the navy to the army, he decided to enlist, thereby obtaining a choice in which branch he would serve. And thankfully, the University of Illinois was very cooperative; since Grandpa had never failed a subject, he was told to go ahead and enlist, and his diploma would be mailed to his home in June. This pleased his mother, but Ralph Jones wasn't very happy. Grandpa finally got Jones to agree that winning in Germany was more important than winning basketball games.

After Grandpa had worked out all of the details confirming his graduation, he went up to the Great Lakes Naval Training Station and enlisted as a Carpenter's Mate Second Class. It didn't take him long to find out that they had an officer's school there, so he applied for admission.

Grandpa and Charlie Bachman, an All-American offensive guard at Notre Dame, entered Officer Candidate School (OCS) at the same time. John "Paddy" Driscoll, a star quarterback at Northwestern, joined them, and they all helped each other get through a tough training course. Grandpa knew nothing about seamanship, except that he had missed being on the *Eastland* when it capsized. Meanwhile, Charlie was a bit weak in math. Yet they worked very hard tutoring each other, and at the end of three months they were commissioned as ensigns. They expected to go right to sea so they could destroy the German navy, but Grandpa soon learned you do what you are told to do in the service.

Grandpa never saw any combat duty at sea. Great Lakes Naval Training Station was very active in sports, so Grandpa's tour of duty consisted of him becoming Great Lakes' recreation officer, which involved playing and coaching football as well as playing basketball and baseball. It may not have helped the war effort against Germany, but playing and coaching for the Great Lakes teams is what he was ordered to do.

While Grandpa was in OCS, the University of Illinois remained true to its promise and sent him his diploma. While on a weekend pass, he returned home to visit his mother and the rest of the family. She had already framed his diploma and hung it next to Walter's on the living room wall. Despite her joy and pride in Grandpa's accomplishment, she was more interested in the day-to-day duties that were assigned to him by the navy.

Grandpa learned the rudiments of seamanship and close-order drill. He pulled watch, which was customary for recruits, but participating in athletics took up a good portion of his time. Grandpa's OCS class had some great athletes, especially on the football team. In addition to Bachman and Driscoll, the squad had Richard Reichle (Illinois), Lawrence Eklund (Minnesota), Emmett Keefe (Notre Dame), Gerald Jones (Notre Dame), Hugh Blacklock (Michigan State), Harold Erickson (St. Olaf), Harry Eileson (Northwestern), Charles "Blondy" Reeves (Ottawa, Ontario, Canada), and Jimmy Conzelman (Washington–St. Louis). All of the men were college stars. Driscoll was recognized as one of the greatest collegiate quarterbacks. The team had a devastating attack with Blacklock at tackle and Reeves and Conzelman at running back. (Driscoll, Conzelman, and Grandpa would all eventually be inducted into the Pro Football Hall of Fame.)

In 1918 Great Lakes defeated just about everybody it played. There were two ties—with Northwestern and Notre Dame—but the squad beat all of its other opponents. One weekend, Grandpa recalled that the Great Lakes team took three trainloads of sailors with it on a trip to play the United States Naval Academy. Those sailors reportedly were busy prior to the game laying bets that Great Lakes would beat Navy.

The Naval Academy scored the game's first touchdown but missed the point after. As the game progressed, big Bill Ingram, Navy's great fullback, was en route to scoring his second touchdown when he was hit on the 1-yard line and fumbled. The ball bounced right into the arms of Harry Eileson, who began running toward the opposite goal line. Although Grandpa and Conzelman were protecting Eileson's rear, someone jumped off the Navy bench and tackled Eileson as he was running downfield. Later, it was believed that the Navy coach was yelling, "Go get him, go get him!" which spurred some youngster on the bench to run out and tackle Eileson at the 40-yard line.

Controversy broke out. Both teams cleared their benches; the Annapolis students ran out on the field and were met by Great Lakes supporters. There was considerable discussion as to whether or not

Great Lakes should be awarded a touchdown. Finally, the admiral who commanded the Naval Academy at the time stepped out on the field to settle the matter. The admiral overruled the officials' decision—that Navy should be penalized half the distance to the goal line—and awarded Great Lakes the touchdown. The touchdown stood up as Great Lakes nipped Navy 7–6.

Another noted game had Great Lakes facing Rutgers. Paul Robeson, who later became a famous singing star in the musical *Showboat*, led Rutgers, which jumped out to a 14–0 lead at the end of the first half. However, early in the third quarter, Rutgers made the mistake of attempting to get rough with the Great Lakes team. Grandpa and his teammates didn't take kindly to it, and took it out on their opponents. The final score: Great Lakes 54, Rutgers 14.

Lieutenant Jay McReavy, an Annapolis graduate, was head coach of the Great Lakes football team. McReavy also commanded the Officers Training School, which was a demanding job in and of itself. One day, Grandpa, Charlie Bachman, and Paddy Driscoll went to their coach and suggested they take charge of the coaching duties and daily practices during the week so McReavy could devote himself to his duties as commanding officer of the school.

This was fine with the lieutenant, and it worked out well for the team. McReavy kept in touch with the trio during the week, and they made certain that he did the actual coaching on Saturdays.

The team's biggest thrill came when it was invited to play the Mare Island Marines in the Rose Bowl on January 1, 1919. The Marines had a crackerjack team that came into the game undefeated at 10–0 with no ties. Great Lakes, meanwhile, had won six games and tied two.

This game was also to serve as the armed forces championship. William "Lone Star" Dietz, the legendary Washington State head coach, coached the Marines, which boasted many stars—the greatest of whom was running back Benton "Biff" Bangs (he helped lead the Cougars to the 1916 Rose Bowl title).

The Mare Island Marines also had one of the greatest centers in the game, Jake Risley. That day, Grandpa thought he played the best game of his life. He was always wary of ever calling himself a star, but on this particular day, Grandpa was a star. His tackling was terrific on defense, and on offense he scored a touchdown on a 45-yard pass from Driscoll. Grandpa also intercepted a pass and ran it back 77 yards to the 3-yard line, where a determined Marine named Jim Blewett nailed him. In retrospect, Grandpa should never have been tackled, and through the years that he coached, he told all his players to dive for the goal line when they reached the 3. Anyone who can't dive three yards, he said, should play cards, not football.

Later, Driscoll found Grandpa again for another apparent touchdown. Paddy threw the ball low, but Grandpa made a shoestring catch…or so he thought. The referee—Walter Eckersall, who played at the University of Chicago—ruled that Grandpa had trapped the ball. Grandpa didn't like the call, but he learned a lesson that he took with him when he eventually became head coach of the Chicago Bears: whenever there was a questionable call, he always worked with an official to help him make the proper call—a formula that worked more often than not in later years.

Great Lakes went on to win 17–0, and Grandpa was named Most Valuable Player. But the real MVP was Paddy Driscoll, who put on a football clinic. He returned punts for a total of 115 yards, rushed for 34 yards (not counting one run that Eckersall called back), punted for an average of 43 yards, and completed four of eight passes—including the 45-yarder that Grandpa caught for a touchdown. Paddy also caught a pass to set up a score, and drop-kicked a field goal from 30 yards out, all while running the offensive flawlessly at quarterback.

The team returned to Great Lakes and received a hero's welcome at its own station. More important, McReavy gave Grandpa and the team a three-day pass, which he used to go see his mother and Min. His mother didn't understand much about football, but the newspapers were full of

Rose Bowl stories, and reading those accounts, she realized it was a great victory.

Her biggest concern was that Grandpa might get hurt playing football. Grandpa tried to put her mind at ease by telling her that he played end, a position that didn't put him in the thick of all the rough stuff. But his mother countered with this question: "If it's so safe, how did you get your jaw and your leg broken at Illinois?"

Well, she had him there, but he told her that his playing days on the gridiron were over, and if he decided to play any sport after the navy, it would be baseball. She was mollified somewhat since Frank and Walter had played baseball and never got hurt. At that point, Grandpa honestly felt the game of football was over for him (of course, at that time he had no idea what the future had in store).

Grandpa continued his duties as a recreation officer until he was discharged following 14 months of active duty. When Grandpa returned home, he felt uneasy about not having made a more serious contribution to the war effort. But when he discussed the situation with his mother, she reassured him by pointing out that he had done exactly what he was ordered to do. Moreover, she said, navy men who had seen him play enjoyed the games. Still, Grandpa resolved that if the nation ever went to war again, he would put on the uniform one more time.

Chapter 3

PLAYING FOR THE YANKEES

New York Yankees scout Bob Connery had paid Grandpa a visit while he was playing outfield for Illinois during his junior year. Connery also came out to see some of the Great Lakes games in which Grandpa had played, and recommended him to the Yankees organization for a tryout. The Yankees invited Grandpa to spring training, and he accepted with alacrity. Camp was held in Jacksonville, Florida, and he was in great condition. Defensively, he was running wild in the outfield; batting, however, was another story.

In one of their spring games, the Yankees played the Brooklyn Dodgers. They were facing Rube Marquard, the famous left-hander. Rube had a devastating curveball, but since this game was being contested early in the spring, Grandpa guessed that Rube would utilize his fastball more (no need for him to risk a sore arm on a rookie). Grandpa was correct. Rube threw him a fastball right down the middle, and Grandpa—a switch-hitter batting right-handed against Marquard—banged it toward the gap between left and center field.

Grandpa never hesitated around first and headed toward second. The ball rolled all the way to the fence, so he kept on going and slid safely into third. However, he injured his hip on the hard ground around the bag. Nonetheless, Grandpa impressed manager Miller Huggins and the rest of the organization enough that when the Yankees broke camp and headed north, he had made the team. Although the hip was still bothering him a great deal, he was confident that the injury would eventually work itself out.

Grandpa's contract with the Yankees was for $400 a month, and he was to receive a $500 bonus for signing. Huggins explained that the bonus would be paid when they reached New York because Jake Ruppert, a brewer who owned the Yankees, liked to pay bonuses personally. Grandpa was happy to make the team, but he felt some guilt because veteran outfielder Ping Bodie, who taught him the finer points of playing outfield in the big leagues, was cut to make room for him.

The hip was still bothering Grandpa on Opening Day at the Polo Grounds in 1919. He did not play until the ninth game of the season. That day, he reached base on a drag-bunt single and played right field.

The next morning Grandpa reported to the Yankees' office. There, Huggins introduced Grandpa to Ruppert, who gave Grandpa his bonus. As Ruppert handed Grandpa the check, he asked, "Young man, what are you going to do with all of this money?"

Grandpa replied, "Mr. Ruppert, I would like to invest this money wisely."

Ruppert beamed and suggested that Huggins speak to his friend, Harry Sinclair of Sinclair Oil, about the best course for Grandpa to take with his bonus money. When Grandpa met Sinclair, he was told that Sinclair Oil was starting to explore for oil in Central America. Sinclair thought Grandpa would do well to join forces with his company in this venture, but Grandpa was initially reluctant to put his entire $700 fortune on the line. In the end, Grandpa decided to risk the entire sum and, as it turned out, Sinclair hit it big, but not in Central America; he ended up striking it rich in South America.

In Grandpa's second major league game, the Yankees faced the Senators at the Polo Grounds. During his first at-bat, he hit a long ball off the great Walter Johnson that had home-run distance, but the ball ended up foul. Had it been fair, the Yanks would have won the game 1–0 in 10 innings. Grandpa was very fortunate because Johnson threw him all fastballs. Johnson was famous for his fastball, but it didn't seem to bother Grandpa because of his experience playing indoor baseball where there is a very short pitching distance. In his next at-bat, he again drove Johnson's first offering into the right-field stands, but again it was foul. After that, Johnson threw Grandpa only curves, and Grandpa was helpless.

Huggins seemed to take an interest in Grandpa because of his switch-hitting abilities, a rare commodity in those days. If the Yankees happened to be losing a game by several runs, Huggins had Grandpa coach third base. The Yankees tried to rest Grandpa and his sore hip as much as possible to give it a chance to heal, so he was in and out of the lineup quite a bit.

Huggins didn't put Grandpa in the lineup when the Yankees went on the road to play Detroit, which boasted Ty Cobb in its batting order. One day, Cobb—whom Grandpa idolized—came up to bat for the Tigers. Yankees pitcher Ernie Shore and catcher Truck Hannah were sitting next to Grandpa in the dugout. They egged Grandpa on with the hope that he would razz Cobb.

Trying to make an impression with his teammates, Grandpa verbally needled Cobb while the Tigers great was batting. Finally, Cobb dropped his bat and came over to the Yankees dugout. Cobb didn't make any overt move toward Grandpa. Instead he said, "Listen, punk, I'll see you after the game. Don't forget it." Grandpa told Cobb that he'd be looking for him, too.

After the game, Grandpa took a shower. The Yankees veterans, anticipating a skirmish between George Halas and Ty Cobb, were dressed and out of the locker room before Grandpa had finished dressing. Finally, Grandpa stepped out of the Yankees dressing room, and Cobb emerged from the Detroit side. Grandpa thought Cobb was going to belt him in the nose, but instead Cobb walked over to Grandpa and stuck out his hand. Cobb said, "I like your spirit, punk, but don't overdo it when you don't have to."

The Yanks got back to New York and were scheduled to host the Tigers this time around. One day, Grandpa walked from his room on 145th and Broadway all the way down to 42nd Street. When he got to 42nd Street, he ran into none other than Ty Cobb. Cobb was very cordial, and they walked over half a mile together. During their stroll, Cobb gave Grandpa a lot of sound advice. He suggested that Grandpa save all his fire for when he stepped onto the baseball diamond and at the same time keep his mouth shut. Cobb pointed out that nobody ever made it in the big leagues with a big mouth.

Many years later, after Cobb had retired and Grandpa was running the Chicago Bears, the team would stay at the Commodore Hotel in Los Angeles and Cobb would always make it a point to come over and visit. Grandpa and Cobb became great friends; Cobb handled Grandpa like the big-leaguer that Cobb was, and Grandpa was always grateful to Cobb for the way he handled things.

The Yankees then traveled to Cleveland for a series, but Grandpa's hip was really bothering him, so he asked Huggins' permission to go to Youngstown to see a man named John D. "Bonesetter" Reese. Reese, who had no formal medical training, was famous in his day for providing remedies for most orthopedic injuries, particularly those of an athletic nature; even *Time* magazine had written about him. When Grandpa had been injured while playing baseball at Illinois, George Huff, the team's manager and the athletics director, sent Grandpa to see Bonesetter Reese on both occasions.

One of Grandpa's injuries had occurred during a fit of anger while playing against Mississippi State. Illinois first baseman Frank English had tripled and Grandpa stepped into the batter's box. All of a sudden, English took off for home despite the fact that there was only one out, and he was out by a mile.

Grandpa was so disgusted and angry over the play that he banged his bat into the ground and popped a tendon in his right arm. Huff sent Grandpa down to see Bonesetter, who went right to work. Bonesetter felt around Grandpa's arm, made a rapid movement, and pressed in. When he did that, he slipped Grandpa's tendon back into the right spot in about two seconds. That was Grandpa's first experience with Bonesetter Reese.

So Grandpa was hoping Bonesetter would produce similar success as he traveled by train to Youngstown to seek help with his ailing hip. It was only an hour-and-a-half ride to Youngstown, and Grandpa figured he could easily make it back to Cleveland Stadium in time for the ballgame because he had confidence Bonesetter could quickly make things right.

When Grandpa got to Bonesetter's office, there was a line of people four deep that stretched around the block. But Grandpa had an appointment, and since Bonesetter was very partial to athletes—especially baseball players—he saw Grandpa immediately. Grandpa was taken into Bonesetter's office and told to strip and lie down on his stomach. Then, Bonesetter dug his fingers into Grandpa's femur and said, "The hip bone is pressing on the nerve."

Bonesetter dug his fingers in as deep as he possibly could without breaking the skin. Then he gave it a twist and said, "Now your hip will be fine."

By the time Grandpa got his clothes back on, he felt 100 percent better. He thanked Bonesetter profusely and hurried back to catch the train. When Grandpa got back to Cleveland for the game that afternoon, he felt like a young colt. During the game, he made a diving catch that delighted Huggins. It seemed as if Grandpa would be a Yankee for a long time.

Following the game, the Yankees headed to Chicago. Grandpa didn't know it that night on the train, but he would be the subject of a nice story by Chicago sportswriter Warren Brown, who chronicled George Halas' return to his hometown and featured Huggins' praise of his new young outfielder. Grandpa was thrilled to learn of the story and that many of his friends would be coming to the game.

That afternoon in Comiskey Park, however, Grandpa did not start in right field against the White Sox. Late in the game, Huggins put Grandpa in to pinch-hit. He faced right-hander Ed Cicotte, whose signature pitch was a knuckleball. The first two pitches Grandpa saw seemed to come right across the plate, then dipped down to the right, yet they held the plate long enough to be called strikes. His third pitch again looked like it was going right over the heart of the plate. Grandpa stepped into the pitch and swung, but it dipped to the right.

He struck out on three pitches.

That night, Huggins called Grandpa in to see him. He thought Grandpa needed more experience, so the Yankees planned to send him to St. Paul of the American Association. Naturally, Grandpa was heartbroken, but he always remembered the way Miller Huggins handled the situation. Whenever Grandpa had to cut a player throughout the years, he tried to emulate Huggins' grace and empathy.

Actually, there was a silver lining to Grandpa no longer being with the Yankees. They sent him to St. Paul with a guaranteed contract, which meant he would getting the same salary he received as a member of the Yankees. He decided to make the best of it, go to St. Paul, and do the best he could.

That same night, Grandpa managed to catch a train to St. Paul, and the next day he reported to Mike Kelly, a man who became his friend as well as a mentor and coach. Kelly was terrific at handling young ballplayers and helping them improve their weaknesses.

A few days after joining the St. Paul squad, Grandpa had a run-in with an umpire, who called a strike on a pitch that had actually sailed over his head. He was furious and began jawing at the umpire, who turned his back on Grandpa and strolled toward first base. Grandpa rushed after the umpire, grabbed his coat sleeve, and shouted, "Listen to me!"

Suddenly, Grandpa realized he had pulled the umpire's sleeve out of his coat and was waving an empty sleeve in the umpire's face. The umpire threw Grandpa out of the game and he was suspended for one game, but the incident worked to his advantage because from that day on, he was one of Kelly's favorites.

Thanks to Kelly's coaching, Grandpa had a pretty good year at St. Paul. At the end of the season, Kelly told Grandpa that he would like him to return to St. Paul the following season. However, St. Paul's pay scale called for a reduction in his salary from $400 a month to $300 a month. The Yankees told him they had a youngster they planned to use in right field named Babe Ruth, but they thought Grandpa would be ready to move up to the parent club after another year of seasoning at St. Paul. Grandpa believed that an additional year with Mike Kelly would prepare him for a return to the big leagues, and he'd certainly stick with the Yankees the second time around.

However, Grandpa reconsidered and concluded he had to make a stand—the Yankees had to decide between him and Ruth. He felt he was ready for the majors. He had a great arm, he was fearless, and Lord knows he had the desire. Faced with a 25 percent pay cut, Grandpa finally decided that it wasn't in his best interests to spend another year playing in St. Paul, so he didn't return. And the Yankees decided to go with Babe Ruth.

Chapter 4

RETURN TO FOOTBALL

With professional baseball no longer in his plans, Grandpa went back to Chicago. He ended up working for the Chicago, Burlington and Quincy Railroad as an engineer in the bridge department, but the desire to compete in the athletic arena still burned in him. Eventually, he learned a semipro football team, the Hammond Pros, was holding tryouts. Grandpa ended up making the team and received $100 per game—a nice chunk of money at that time. But he would learn some lessons in his first game with the Pros that proved to be invaluable years later in professional football.

The Pros squared off against Canton in their first game, and it proved to be a rather enervating initiation into professional football. Canton featured Olympic medal winner and legendary all-around athlete Jim Thorpe, but Hammond fullback Gil Falcon wasn't intimidated at all by Thorpe's presence. He bulled right into Thorpe, who ended up crashing into the bench after their collision. A dazed Thorpe suffered a cut over his right eye, but he got the cut taken care of and didn't miss a down.

On the very next play, Thorpe lowered his left shoulder and knocked Falcon about three feet into the air. The officials had to stop play once again—this time to get Falcon back on his feet.

Canton beat the Pros 7–0 that day, and to no one's surprise, Thorpe ended up scoring the game's only touchdown. The Pros were presented with one scoring opportunity that could have tied the game, but Thorpe made a big play to thwart that scoring chance, and his play made a lasting impression on Grandpa. Hammond had managed to get to the Canton 1-yard line and faced fourth down. Grandpa was playing right end; his job was to take Canton's left tackle out of the play, which he managed to do. He expected Falcon to power right through the hole for what would have been a sure touchdown. However, Thorpe—exhibiting an amazing sixth sense—seemed to know exactly where the play was going. He came up hard from his defensive post, threw his body into Falcon, and knocked him back to the 2-yard line.

Thorpe often didn't use his arms to tackle an opposing ball carrier. He just rammed his body into the runner and was always able to take an opponent down. It proved to be his trademark. He wore special shoulder pads that had a layer of sheet metal in them. Putting sheet metal in shoulder pads was illegal, but Thorpe was playing several games each week all over the country in an effort to capitalize on his famous name. Because the league benefited from Thorpe's presence, teams tended to look the other way and allowed Thorpe to bend the rules a bit.

Grandpa recalled that it was quite a thrill to play against Thorpe, but he also was thrilled to pocket the $100 Hammond paid him for his professional debut. At that time, he sought some financial security, and the money he received was more than twice the amount he made working an entire week at the railroad.

All told, Grandpa played between six and seven games for Hammond that fall, and the paycheck he received each week really got him excited about professional football. Hammond featured a number of outstanding players. Bert Baston from Minnesota played left end while Grandpa played right end. Paddy Driscoll, Grandpa's teammate at Great Lakes, also played for the Pros. Driscoll only weighed about 160 pounds, but he was a nifty runner and was as tough as anyone on the field. He also was a great punter and drop-kicker who could put the ball through the uprights from distances of over 50 yards.

During his last game of the season with Hammond, Grandpa dislocated his clavicle, but his injury didn't diminish the enthusiasm that was building in his mind about professional football. Although he wasn't totally convinced, Grandpa reasoned that if semipro football could attract players like Baston and Driscoll, there might be a future for professional football.

Grandpa's mother, however, didn't share his enthusiasm for football—college, semipro, professional, or otherwise. Baseball was all right, but football worried her. She kept telling him, "George, you're going to get hurt." But Grandpa laughed it off and told her that his main interest was putting his engineering degree to work with the CB&Q and that he'd be going back to baseball the following spring.

Truth be told, Grandpa wasn't really thrilled about pursuing a career in engineering. He worked in an open area in the CB&Q office, figuring stresses and strains on bridges that were going to be built. When he'd look across the room, he could see men 60 years old sitting in their glass-enclosed cubicles doing the same work he was doing. The thought struck him that they had probably been there all of their lives—a prospect that didn't appeal to him very much.

But early in 1920, G.E. Chamberlain, general superintendent of the Staley Starch Company in Decatur, Illinois, approached Grandpa about an opportunity that would eventually change the course of his life. Chamberlain outlined for Grandpa the marvelous opportunities that existed in the starch business; how they took qualified young people and moved them from one department to another to teach them the entire operation so that someday they would be company executives.

Chamberlain told Grandpa that he had come to see him at the behest of A.E. Staley, the company's owner. Chamberlain grabbed Grandpa's attention when he pointed out that Staley was an enthusiastic supporter of athletics. The Staley Company was eager to enhance the starch business by developing the very best company teams in baseball, basketball, and football.

Grandpa asked Chamberlain what his responsibilities with the company would be, and Chamberlain informed him that he would serve as the firm's athletics director. He would play for, coach, and—most importantly—recruit players for the company football team. Chamberlain also said Grandpa would have an opportunity to play with their outstanding baseball team, which was really a semipro team. Joe "Iron Man" McGinnity, who eventually was inducted into the National Baseball Hall of Fame, managed the Staley Starch team.

Chamberlain assured Grandpa that the Staley Company would keep him busy on a year-round basis. Chamberlain told him he could play basketball for the company team, then play baseball for McGinnity during the summer as well as run the football team and perform his duties as athletics director in the fall. At the same time, Chamberlain assured Grandpa he would be given an opportunity to learn the starch business.

Grandpa faced a monumental decision. He was very impressed with what he saw of semipro football during his year with the Hammond Pros, and he also realized that bridge building at the CB&Q wasn't for him. At the same time, he wondered about the wisdom of getting into the starch business. In the end, his mother's concern about security made the possibility of working at the Staley Company a great prospect. He knew that he would have no trouble selling her on participating in sports if he was learning the starch business as well.

So after weighing all his options, Grandpa decided to go to Decatur that spring in time to play baseball for Joe McGinnity. The Yankees might have Babe Ruth in right field, but Iron Man McGinnity was going to get George Halas.

When Grandpa arrived in Decatur, he found there was a great deal to learn about the starch business. His first job was to unload freights of corn. He would weigh each boxcar containing the corn, unload the corn, and then weigh the empty car.

Shortly after Grandpa settled in at the starch company, McGinnity announced that practice for the baseball team was about to begin. Grandpa reported to McGinnity and prepared himself to represent Staley on the diamond that season. A.E. Staley saw to it that the team's field, Staley Park, was in mint condition. The Decatur Staleys played their first game in April, and through May they were playing before 3,000 people who jammed into the park.

By mid-June, Grandpa was batting .326 and playing outfield on a regular basis. He enjoyed playing for McGinnity and always gave him his best effort. McGinnity, in turn, appreciated Grandpa's efforts and named him captain of the squad.

On June 19, a local jeweler announced he would give wristwatches to the first two players who hit homers in their game that day against the Havoline Nine. One of Grandpa's teammates socked a home run early in the game, so only one watch remained. Grandpa was determined to get that other watch, so he belted one out, too.

But that wasn't the end of local businesses offering incentives to members of the Staleys. A men's clothing retailer offered to give a $22 custom-made silk shirt to players for every triple or home run. Throughout the rest of the summer, Grandpa went on a rampage at the plate and added to his wardrobe handsomely. By the time the season ended, he had acquired 17 silk shirts!

Although Grandpa was playing baseball and working at the starch plant, he was laying the groundwork for the Decatur Staleys football team. He and Jake Lanum, who would become one of the team's starting running backs, took off on a weeklong scouting trip, calling on people they knew at various Big Ten schools. They ended up landing some outstanding players.

The first player they signed was Edward "Dutch" Sternaman, a favorite in Decatur because residents supported the University of Illinois and Dutch scored a touchdown that enabled Illinois to beat Ohio State and win the Big Ten championship in 1919. They also signed Bob Koehler, a big fullback at Northwestern.

By the end of June, they had secured the services of Decatur native Kile MacWherter, another fullback, and halfback Walter Veach.

Then in July, they added George Trafton, a center from Notre Dame who eventually would be named to the Pro Football Hall of Fame (Trafton is credited with being the first center to snap the ball with one hand). Another important acquisition followed with the signing of Jimmy Conzelman, Grandpa's teammate on the Rose Bowl–winning Great Lakes team.

It turned out to be a busy summer. Not only was Grandpa learning the starch business and playing baseball, but recruiting also took up a great deal of his time. However, the Staley Company made the recruiting process easier because it was able to offer a package deal that included a year-round job with the company and a share of the profits from the team's gate receipts.

Scheduling games for the Staleys' inaugural season was also time-consuming. Because no organized league existed, if a team wanted to play another club, it proposed a date and hoped it would be mutually acceptable to the opponent. There was a great deal of corresponding back and forth. In a letter to Ralph Hay, who managed the Canton Bulldogs, Grandpa pointed out that it would be ideal for some of the best teams to form a professional league.

The idea of forming a league first entered Grandpa's mind following a conversation he had with Jim Thorpe after Hammond played Canton the previous fall. Thorpe and Grandpa walked off the field together, and Thorpe said, "Pretty nice crowd here."

Grandpa agreed. "Yes, maybe we ought to have a get-together and form some kind of a league. We could really build this into something."

Hay was intrigued with Grandpa's suggestion about forming a league, so he asked Grandpa and managers from 10 of the leading professional teams in the country to meet him at his automobile agency in Canton on September 17, 1920.

The meeting was very informal. There were no chairs or sofas available that day, so all the team managers leaned against cars as they discussed forming the new league. Grandpa recalled that he sat on a running board the entire meeting.

Managers agreed that the league would be named the American Professional Football Association—the predecessor to today's National Football League. Thorpe was elected the league's first president—he also would continue to play for Canton—and franchises were awarded after teams paid a $100 fee. Eleven teams became members of the new Association: the Akron Pros, Canton Bulldogs, Cleveland Tigers, Dayton Triangles, Decatur Staleys, Hammond Pros, Massillon Tigers, Muncie Flyers, Racine Cardinals, Rochester Jeffersons, and Rock Island Independents. The Columbus Panhandles, Buffalo All-Americans, Chicago Tigers, and Detroit Heralds were allowed into the league shortly thereafter, while Massillon later withdrew.

Pro football franchises were not the soundest business investments back then. In fact, of all the original Association teams, only two—the Racine Cardinals (now the Arizona Cardinals) and the Decatur Staleys (now the Chicago Bears)—have survived to this day.

Teams were able to schedule a very tentative slate of games that could provide them with at least eight contests for the upcoming season. League rules stated that teams could not tamper with players already on college or university squads. Grandpa, of course, abided by that rule but was able to assemble quite a team nonetheless.

In addition to the aforementioned players, the Staleys signed Walter Pearce, who had been quarterback at the University of Pennsylvania; Guy Chamberlin, an All-American end from Nebraska; and offensive lineman Andy Feichtinger from Portland. They also signed Millikin teammates Roy Adkins, Randy Young, Jake Lanum, and outstanding fullback Kile MacWherter, along with Leo Johnson and Charley Dressen—a holdover from the Staley team the year before. They obtained Jerry Jones and Hugh Blacklock from Notre Dame and Great Lakes, respectively, as well as Illinois products Ross Petty and Bert Ingwersen, a top tackle. All in all, the Staleys had a solid nucleus of players, and Grandpa was eager to get started.

On Sunday, October 3, the Staleys opened their season before 2,000 fans at Staley Field against the Moline Tractors, who were not in the league. The Staleys' opening lineup is worth noting: Feichtinger at left end, Ingwersen at left tackle, Petty at left guard, Trafton at center, Jones at right guard, Blacklock at right tackle, Halas at right end, Pearce at quarterback, Sternaman at left halfback, Lanum at right halfback, and Koehler at fullback.

Dutch Sternaman scored three touchdowns that day, and Hugh Blacklock kicked two extra points as the Staleys won 20–0. Grandpa's old adversary, Walter Eckersall, the great University of Chicago star, happened to be the referee that day.

The following Sunday, the Staleys handed the Kewanee Walworths a 25–7 loss. Then the Staleys traveled to Rock Island to play the Independents in their first Association game. They managed to beat Rock Island 7–0 thanks to a 43-yard touchdown run by Conzelman. The win over Rock Island before 5,000 people was huge because it established the Staleys as a force to be reckoned with in the new league. The Staleys did have an advantage in that they were able to practice two hours per day on company time, while other teams in the league practiced only when they could. This provided Grandpa's team with split-second precision that its opponents were not able to develop.

When they went to play the Independents, the Staleys were concerned about the reliability of Rock Island's management. The Staleys had a $3,000 guarantee, but they demanded the money be paid to them before they played the game. That night on the train back to Decatur, Grandpa stored the money in his sock, then stuffed the sock into his pillow when he got home. He learned that trick from baseball Hall of Famer Frank "Home Run" Baker while he and Baker were teammates with the Yankees. The Yankees happened to be making a trip to Boston, and after the train stopped, team members hurriedly piled out of the train at one of the suburban Boston stations. Grandpa had put his money in his pillow, but in his rush to get off the train, he forgot the money. Baker said, "Son, I want to teach you a little trick so you won't lose your money. Always put your wallet in your sock and then put it in your pillow. That way, you'll never forget because you'll always be looking for that second sock."

While running the Staleys and playing on the team was Grandpa's main occupation, the people at Staley continued to help him advance within the company. They told him that after he learned everything there was to learn about weighing corn, he would then go into the chemistry department. Grandpa had taken chemistry at Illinois, so he was very happy to hear that the chemistry department was an option. The company then moved him to the glucose department. Midway through the football season, he advanced from the glucose to the starch department.

As the Staleys moved through their schedule, A.E. Staley's enthusiasm for the team grew by leaps and bounds. The players were also excited: they were being paid to play football and were also on the company payroll.

On October 24, accompanied by 200 loyal fans, the Staleys made a trip north to battle the Chicago Tigers at Cubs Park (later known as Wrigley Field). Despite rainy and cold conditions, 5,000 spectators turned out for this matchup. The Staleys managed to beat the Cardinals 10–0, thanks to a sensational 55-yard touchdown run by Pearce. Conzelman's drop-kick field goal provided the final score.

The Staleys enjoyed a remarkable 1920 season, finishing 10–1–2. They played Rock Island to a scoreless tie in their second contest of the year and also battled the Akron Pros to a scoreless tie in the season finale. The Staleys' only loss came at the hands of the Cardinals in a game they lost 7–6. The remarkable thing in Grandpa's mind was that in 13 games, they scored 164 points, held opponents to just 21 points, and shut out 10 of their 13 foes.

Grandpa always liked to tell a story about one of the games with Rock Island. The Independents had a good fullback who could really fly humorously named Fred Chicken. On one play, Trafton tackled Chicken and knocked him into a wooden fence that bordered the field, breaking Chicken's leg in the process.

Rock Island's team physician certainly had his work cut out for him that day as the Staleys knocked out three other Independent players within the next five minutes. Grandpa wasn't sure seeing three more Rock Island players go down was the best thing for his team, considering the Staleys were playing on Rock Island's home field. The hometown fans were not pleased. People started hollering from the stands about what was going to happen to the Staleys—and Trafton, in particular—after the game.

Late in the game, Trafton approached Grandpa and asked him to call a timeout. He told Grandpa he was sorry, but he couldn't stay for the end of the game. He believed the Rock Island fans were going to mob him.

Grandpa managed to calm Trafton down as best he could and suggested that as soon as the gun sounded to end the game, Trafton should start running to the Staleys bench, and the rest of the team would cover for him. Trafton hemmed and hawed, but finally agreed to finish the game. Grandpa felt the Staleys needed Trafton because he was the bulwark of their line.

When the final gun went off, Trafton started running for the Staleys bench. When he got there, the team trainer, Andy Lotshaw, told Trafton to put on a sweatshirt in order to cover his number so the Rock Island

George Trafton was inducted into the Pro Football Hall of Fame in 1964.

fans wouldn't recognize him. Trafton pulled the sweatshirt over his jersey, but he still thought he might need a little extra protection, so he grabbed a milk bottle the team was using to draw water from a bucket and started out of the park.

Lotshaw had a cab waiting for Trafton, who crawled into the cab not a minute too soon as rocks thrown by Rock Island fans crashed right through the cab's windows. Trafton didn't know what to do. He got out of the other side of the cab and started running down the road toward the Illinois-Iowa state line.

He had run about half a mile when a car pulled alongside of him.

The driver said, "Where are you going in such a hurry, kid?"

"Davenport," Trafton replied.

The driver said, "Jump in."

Trafton got into the car and rode with the fellow across the state line to Davenport, Iowa, in his football uniform.

An overnight train ride to Minneapolis that season produced another memory for Grandpa that taught him how to better handle his players. The Staleys had scheduled a game against the Minneapolis Marines. The team boarded a train at about 9:00 that evening and took over an entire car. One of the players started a game of dice in the men's room, with seven or eight players taking part. Many of the players on the squad were older than Grandpa, but he felt he had to figure out a way to exercise his authority as coach and get them to bed before midnight.

Rather than lay down the law and break up the game, however, he ended up joining the action. He reasoned that if he played along with them for a while, they would be more receptive when he asked them to hit the sack before midnight. He lost money that evening, but the players followed his instruction. It was a huge relief for Grandpa, and the Staleys ended up winning the game the next day 3–0 on a Dutch Sternaman field goal.

The season's final contest against Akron—which proved to be the American Professional Football Association's first championship game—certainly was the Staleys' best-played game of the year despite the fact that it ended in a 0–0 tie. Grandpa wanted a rematch with Akron, but it refused to play another game. Paddy Driscoll, who played with Grandpa both at Hammond and on the Great Lakes team, suited up for the Staleys that day. Grandpa hoped to obtain Driscoll's services that fall, and the two had a verbal agreement. But prior to the season, Driscoll had second thoughts and signed with the Racine Cardinals, who agreed to give him $3,000 for 10 games. He was only allowed to play for the Staleys in this one game because his contract with Racine had concluded for the season.

The Racine Cardinals were started up by Chris O'Brien, a painting and decorating contractor, along with his brother Pat. The team started off as a neighborhood club that played on the southwest side of Chicago. They were first known as the Morgan Athletic Club and played their games at Normal Park, located at 61st Street and Racine. Later, the team changed its name to the Racine Cardinals after Chris O'Brien purchased used jerseys for his team that were faded maroon. Looking at the jerseys, O'Brien insisted they were Cardinal red, not maroon, prompting the name change.

The Cardinals handed the Staleys their only loss earlier in the season, but the Staleys managed to get the Cardinals back on the field a week later, and the Staleys beat them 10–0.

At season's end, each member of the team received around $1,900 as his share of the gate receipts. Since Grandpa was also the coach, the team voted him an extra share of the gate, which was perfectly fine with him.

The Staley Company had been very good to the entire football team, and especially good to Grandpa. In addition to his athletic duties, he was in line for a promotion in the near future.

And Grandpa's personal life was looking up, as well. He asked his biggest fan, Min, to marry him and she said yes. Grandpa found himself looking at houses because Min was excited about the possibility of settling down in Decatur. Back in Chicago, Grandpa's mother couldn't be happier that her youngest son had, at last, found job security with the Staley Starch Company.

The country soon found itself in an economic depression, however, and the effects hit the Staley Company hard. One day, Mr. Staley called Grandpa into his office and told him that out of necessity, he had to curtail the company's athletics program. He said it wasn't fair for the company to pay salaries to athletes practicing and playing football during a time of economic hardship.

However, it was obvious to Mr. Staley that football piqued Grandpa's interest more than starch. Staley told Grandpa that Chicago would serve as a much better base for professional football than Decatur due to its size and its ability to draw larger crowds to the games. So he offered Grandpa the opportunity to bring the team to Chicago and assume ownership of the club. Furthermore, Staley gave Grandpa $5,000 to help get him started.

Grandpa was overwhelmed, to say the least, at the generosity of Mr. Staley's offer. Staley made only one request: that Grandpa would agree to call the team the Staleys for one more year.

Grandpa asked Staley to give him a couple of days to think about it. He hurried to Chicago on the first train he could catch and went to see Bill Veeck Sr., then the president of the Chicago Cubs. Grandpa told Veeck about bringing the Staleys to Chicago, and asked him if he would be willing to allow them to play their home games at Cubs Park. Veeck indicated he would meet with Cubs officials to discuss Grandpa's proposal, but looked favorably on the idea.

The Cubs' season was finished and the park wasn't being used on Sundays. Grandpa was confident enough in Veeck's response that he hurried back to Decatur to meet with Mr. Staley once more.

The next day Grandpa thanked him profusely. Grandpa accepted his offer and immediately began to make plans to move the team to Chicago. This time, there wouldn't be any headline heralding the return of Halas to his hometown. This time, the road ahead promised only hard work.

"Pull up your socks, Halas, and tighten your chinstrap," Grandpa told himself. "We're going to Chicago."

Chapter 5

THE BIRTH
OF THE BEARS

The year 1921 turned out to be noteworthy for the Staleys and Grandpa in their first season playing in Chicago. The Staleys compiled a 9–1–1 record in the American Professional Football League—it had changed its name from Association to League in 1921—and this time around there was no disputing that they had won the league championship. Although the Staleys found themselves financially in the red by a tiny amount—$71.63—they were entering a new year full of optimism.

Grandpa and Bill Veeck Sr. finalized a deal that would enable the team to play its home games at Cubs Park. Grandpa was very much a Cubs fan, and he wanted to honor Veeck and the Cubs in some way. Since the team was no longer obligated to call itself the Staleys, Grandpa first decided he wanted to call the team the Cubs. But after concluding that football players were much larger than baseball players, he decided to name his team the Bears.

In 1922, the American Professional Football League underwent another name change. From then on it would be known as the National

Football League, and the league granted Chicago a franchise with its new name, the Bears. Grandpa decided he needed help running the team, so he made Dutch Sternaman an equal partner. He also hoped to make his old friend, Paddy Driscoll, an equal partner with him and Sternaman—each would have one-third stock in the club—if Driscoll could play for the Bears as well. However, Driscoll was still property of their rivals, the Racine Cardinals (who changed their name to the Chicago Cardinals in 1922 after a team from Racine, Wisconsin, joined the NFL). Joe Carr, the president of the league, insisted that Driscoll's contract with the Cardinals be upheld, so he refused to allow Driscoll to join the Bears.

Although the Bears were not able to obtain Driscoll, they did land one player who would prove to be very valuable for several seasons. When the Staleys faced the Rock Island Independents in 1921, Grandpa lined up at right end against Rock Island's Ed Healey, who at that time was considered to be a giant at 220 pounds. Healey had a so-so career at

The Original "Monsters of the Midway"

The University of Chicago once fielded a formidable football team in the Big Ten Conference. Amos Alonzo Stagg, one of football's all-time great innovators, coached for 41 years (from 1892 through 1932) at the University of Chicago, which was a national power at that time.

The Maroons actually were the original "Monsters of the Midway." Midway is a reference to a street called Midway Plaisance, which ran through the center of campus.

The university president decided to drop the school's football program in 1939, and the Bears applied "Monsters of the Midway" to their team as they began to dominate the NFL in 1940 and 1941. The Maroons left the Big Ten in 1946.

Dartmouth, but he really found himself when he entered the professional ranks.

Healey proved to be too much for Grandpa to handle. On one play, Grandpa stepped forward as the ball was snapped, and held Healey for a fraction of a second, enabling Sternaman to gain seven yards through a hole that Grandpa made by holding Healey. Healey jumped up and hollered, "Holding! You were holding me, Halas! If you do that again, I'll knock your block off."

They called the same play again, and again, Grandpa held Healey. But Grandpa got knocked down to his hands and knees in the process. Good thing he did, because his head moved out of the way just as Healey's big fist went right past it. Healey's momentum was so great that he fell, and his hand got buried into the muddy field right up to his wrist.

Grandpa jumped up, ran over to the referee, and yelled, "Healey's holding me. He punched me. Throw him out of the game." Healey yelled at the official just as loud and said he was going to get even with Grandpa somehow.

Grandpa knew Healey was a fine tackle, and he had great admiration for his spirit. The thought entered his mind that he would love to have Healey play for the Bears.

As it turned out, Rock Island owed the Bears $100. Grandpa told the Rock Island management he'd call it even if it would give Healey to the Bears. Rock Island agreed, and Grandpa was very happy that it did. Healey became a Pro Football Hall of Famer and one of the greatest tackles that the NFL has ever seen. Grandpa and Healey formed a friendship that would last throughout the rest of their lives.

In one year, Grandpa landed a great player, was part of a new, exciting football league...and became a newlywed. He married Min on February 18, 1922. Almost immediately after their marriage, my grandmother started working in the Bears' office three days a week, sometimes as many as five. In addition to her clerical duties, she started compiling scrapbooks that she kept all of her life. Every day, she would go through the newspaper, hoping to find some reference to the Bears. When she did, she clipped it out and threw it into an old bread box. Then during the off-season, she would paste these clippings into what became an annual scrapbook.

My grandmother, Min Halas

In 1922, the NFL and its major teams were not yet clearly established. There were more than 12 semipro teams that had their own following; many of these teams drew 1,000 or 2,000 fans who were not attending Bears games. Chicago was home to three NFL clubs: the Bears, the Cardinals, and the Tigers. The Bears played on the north side, while the Cardinals and Tigers played on the south side.

The city could no longer support three teams, so the Cardinals and Tigers agreed to play a game to determine which team would represent the south side. The winner of the game would continue to play in the NFL; the losing team would disband. The Chicago Cardinals won the contest and would become the Bears' principal rival over the next several years. (The Tigers disbanded after the 1920 season.)

Grandpa realized that changing the attitude of sports fans would not happen overnight. In order to drum up support and publicity for the Bears, and to convince the general public that the quality of NFL football was superior to semipro teams, Grandpa and Sternaman made the rounds to Chicago newspaper offices.

College football coaches constantly ridiculed professional football. Grandpa recalled Knute Rockne talking about how any good college team could beat any good pro team because college players were in great condition while pro players were just old men. Yet many college players who had gained great reputations tried the pro game for a short period of time, and fans who had cheered them on in college took interest in them as pros. Many times, when a college coach or newspaper reporter deplored the fact that a college star had succumbed to climbing the professional money tree, they made very derogatory statements that tilted public opinion in their favor. However, Grandpa always felt that even if you are being misrepresented, it's better to have your name mentioned than to be ignored.

In order to generate more favorable press, Grandpa hired Eddie Geiger, a reporter for the *Evening Post* and later for the *Chicago American*, as the Bears' first public relations man. Well, Grandpa didn't exactly hire him as an official PR guy. He paid Geiger $25 per game to do write-ups, which he then took to all of the newspapers in the hope they would print the story.

Grandpa also took other measures to sell NFL football to the city of Chicago, such as giving away tickets. He invited anyone he met to see a Bears game as his guest. But despite his efforts to give away tickets, the Bears managed a top crowd of only 12,000. Grandpa once again talked to Paddy Driscoll because he thought Paddy could help fill a lot of those empty seats, but Joe Carr again would not allow Driscoll to join the Bears.

Despite not being able to land Driscoll, the Bears added several players that year. They inked Sternaman's kid brother, Joey, who had an outstanding career as a quarterback at Illinois. Then Dutch and Grandpa went to their old stomping ground, Notre Dame, and obtained center Ojay Larson, tackle Hector Garvey, and guard Hartley "Hunk" Anderson, who began what would be a long association with the Bears. Also at that time, Grandpa's brother Frank started his duties as the Bears' traveling secretary—a job he held for 50 years.

Prior to the season, the Bears trained at Logan Square Park. They'd practice in the morning, take an hour for lunch, then hit the field again in the afternoon. Usually, each team member gulped down a couple of sandwiches and an apple; if they wanted something to drink other than water, they'd have to wait for the milkman to drive by and buy a pint of milk from him. All they had at the park was a shed for dressing, and the entire squad shared just one shower. However, money was very tight in those days, so Grandpa and the team made the most of their practice facilities. In fact, to make ends meet, Grandpa had to get a job as night watchman at the Bushing Ice Plant—the plant was owned by my grandmother's family—while Dutch worked at a gas station.

The Bears played 12 games in 1922, winning nine, losing three, and finishing second in the league to Canton. Arguably, their biggest wins were over the Oorang Indians—a traveling team from LaRue, Ohio, that featured Jim Thorpe—and the Rock Island Independents. They beat Thorpe's club 33–6 and beat Rock Island twice, 10–6 and 3–0. Two of their three losses were close games: they fell to Canton 7–6 and to the Cardinals 6–0.

The team turned a net profit of $1,476.92 that year. Grandpa and Dutch were offered $35,000 for the franchise, but they turned it down. Despite Grandpa's enthusiasm over the team's season and their finances, he still wasn't able to persuade his mother that pro football was a stable endeavor. "Go back to the railroad, George," she suggested at a family dinner meeting. "There you'll have a good future and a steady job." But by this time, it was too late to return to the railroad. Football was fast becoming a way of life for Grandpa.

The 1923 campaign mirrored the Bears' first NFL season. They finished 9–2–1 and once again placed second to Canton. They really should have won 10 games, but the Milwaukee Badgers tied them in the next-to-last game of the year. Dutch and Grandpa were coaching the Bears as well as playing.

Probably the most important game they played that season was against Oorang, a team formed by Walter Lingo. He owned the Oorang dog kennels in LaRue—a town about 50 miles north of Columbus—and used the team for marketing purposes. Airedale dogs were very popular in those days, and Lingo raised them commercially. He would invite famous athletes and celebrities of that era to LaRue to go hunting with him and his dogs.

One of those famous athletes was Thorpe, with whom Lingo became friends. Lingo actually spoke several Native American languages and studied American history. He also was crazy about football, so both he and Thorpe came up with the idea of forming a team comprised of Native American players. Grandpa recalled that Lingo recruited players primarily from Carlisle and Haskell, two schools that the government created, as well as from Chippewa reservations in Wisconsin and Minnesota.

The Indians had players on their team named Black Bear, Red Fang, Little Twig, and Deer Slayer. But the team also boasted Thorpe and halfback Joe Guyon—both of whom were eventually inducted into the Pro Football Hall of Fame.

During the Bears' matchup against Oorang, an Indians player named Gray Horse fumbled as the Indians were about to go over the Bears' goal line. The ball plopped right into Grandpa's hands and he ran it back for what was to become a longstanding-NFL-record 98-yard touchdown. It seemed more like 198 yards, because Jim Thorpe was running after Grandpa. Grandpa didn't want to be on the receiving end of one of Thorpe's patented body-crushing tackles, so he kept Thorpe off-balance by zigzagging his way to the end zone.

Actually, the Bears didn't have much trouble with the Indians that day as they won 26–0. Rock Island and the champion Canton Bulldogs handed them their only losses of the year, 3–0 and 6–0, respectively.

In early January 1924, NFL clubs held a meeting and made the following resolutions: visiting teams were guaranteed a minimum of $1,200 per game; there would be no compensation if the game was canceled; and game officials would receive $35 for working a game, plus expenses.

Since the Canton Bulldogs had won the championship in 1923, the league voted to give each player an engraved football while the team received a pennant. The engraved footballs cost around $10 each, while each pennant ran between $37 and $50.

The NFL held another meeting in late July and decided that anyone who applied for a franchise in the future must post $500 up front. Joe Carr's salary was raised to $1,000 per year, while the league's secretary received a similar amount. The league also decided that $100 of the $1,200 guarantee given to visiting teams each game was to be used for hotel and travel expenses. Visiting teams also were offered the option of receiving 40 percent of the gross rather than the guarantee after 15 percent had been taken off the top for rent.

In addition to their coaching and playing duties, Dutch and Grandpa continued to recruit players, schedule games, fix equipment, and sell (or give away) tickets. Although most people in those days had not gone to college, fans were more aware of the college game than of professional football. Grandpa believed working-class people and their families could develop a similar loyalty to the Bears. One intangible that Grandpa thought the Bears had going for them was the fact that even if a working man liked a particular college team, it would be difficult for him to attend the games since they were always played on Saturdays (everyone usually worked six days a week). So Grandpa reasoned that if he could get average working men and their families interested in a team that played on their day off (Sunday), he and the Bears would be in business.

Grandpa and Dutch beefed up the Bears' roster prior to the 1924 season by adding more players. Merrill Taft, a big fullback from Wisconsin, joined the team, along with James Leonard, a tackle who captained the Colgate team. They already had proven outstanding tackles such as Blacklock, Scott, and Healey, so the acquisition of Leonard made the Bears even stronger at that particular position. At left end, there were Frank Hanny and Verne Mullen, who played for the Bulldogs the previous year. Grandpa manned right end, of course. The Bears also welcomed Jim McMillen—an outstanding guard from Illinois who also was an excellent wrestler—to the team.

Although the team gained strength on the playing field, its financial situation was constantly in peril. For example, in 1922 the players' salaries amounted to $18,315, and renting the ballpark cost just over $9,000. Receipts from the games amounted to nearly $74,000, which left the Bears with a net profit of $1,476.92.

However, 1923 was another story. Although their gate receipts jumped to nearly $81,000 (they didn't purchase any new players), the rental of the ballpark increased to $12,604.83, and the Bears absorbed a bottom-line loss of $366.72. They managed to offset the loss somewhat with the interest on bank deposits ($20.10), the selling of a player ($175), and other income ($295.10). Profits from the 1924 season again brought them up to a credit line of $1,988.14.

But the Bears' bottom line was about to improve dramatically in 1925. The reason? The arrival of Red Grange, a native of Wheaton—located just 30 miles west of Chicago—whose stellar career at the University of Illinois captured nationwide attention. Grange, truly a one-man show, took his place with the sports immortals of that day such as Babe Ruth, Bobby Jones, Jack Dempsey, and Gene Tunney.

In October 1925, Frank Zambrino, who had a movie distributorship on Wabash Avenue in Chicago, approached Grandpa and told him about his friend C.C. Pyle, who was running a movie theater in Champaign— hometown of the University of Illinois where Grange was finishing up his final college season.

Pyle was attempting to become Grange's manager. Zambrino asked Grandpa if in the event Pyle did become Grange's manager, whether Grandpa was interested in having Grange play for the Bears. Well, you can guess Grandpa's response!

Pyle called Grange into his office. He and Grange worked out a deal that would have him play in the Bears' final two games of 1925 after he had played his final game at Illinois. When the Bears finished their season, Grange and the Bears would then embark on a cross-country tour of cities interested in seeing him play. Pyle told Grange the deal would put $100,000 in Grange's pocket, guaranteed.

Grange agreed, so Pyle met Zambrino, Dutch, and Grandpa in Chicago to discuss the details. Dutch and Grandpa were on their guard, but figured they had nothing to lose by listening to Pyle's proposal. Their meeting took place at the Morrison Hotel in a rather elaborate suite that Pyle had reserved. Dutch and Grandpa offered Pyle and Grange one-third of the net profits for the tour if they could sign Grange, but Pyle had other ideas. He thought the Bears should get one-third, while he and Grange received two-thirds.

Negotiations with Pyle extended over a 26-hour period. When the smoke cleared, Dutch and Grandpa hammered out an agreement with Pyle that enabled the Bears to keep one-half of the receipts from the tour, while the Bears paid all expenses. The Bears signed Grange right after his final game with Illinois on a Saturday, and he was in uniform for the Bears' game the next day, although he didn't see any action.

The city buzzed with excitement over Grange becoming a Bear. The Monday before a Thanksgiving Day game against the Cardinals, Grandpa received a phone call from a friend, Charley Sidebottom, who was working for A.G. Spalding Company at 211 South State Street. He insisted Grandpa rush over to his office because pandemonium had broken loose. To his amazement, Grandpa saw a line of people four abreast down State Street, down Monroe, back up Wabash, and around the block. They were all waiting for tickets to see Red Grange play. Grandpa was thrilled.

Grange entered the Bears' lineup that Thanksgiving Day, just five days after he had played his final collegiate game against Ohio State. A crowd of 39,000 jammed Cubs Park, and it was estimated that 30,000 more fans were turned away at the gate.

Another 28,000 attended Grange's second game. Grandpa couldn't explain the drop-off in attendance; it may have been due to the fact that there had been a snowstorm that day and that everyone had rushed out to see Grange's first game. In any case, Grange accounted for 140 total yards as the Bears edged Columbus 14–13.

On December 2, Grange put on a clinic against the Donnelley All-Stars in St. Louis. He scored four touchdowns as the Bears won handily 39–6. Since St. Louis' owner was a mortician, one of the sportswriters suggested that some of the All-Stars must have been Donnelley's clients.

*Red Grange
put professional
football on
the map
barnstorming
with the Bears in
1925.*

The Bears then went on to Philadelphia to play the Frankford Yellow Jackets on December 5. An estimated 40,000 filled the seats, even though an entire section was empty because someone in the Yellow Jackets ticket office held back 300 seats in the upper grandstand and forgot to sell them. Grange scored two touchdowns and the Bears defeated the home team 14–7.

There was no rest for Grange and the Bears as they traveled to the Polo Grounds to face the New York Giants. The Polo Grounds hosted the annual Army-Navy game the day before, so overflow crowd seating was already set up. It's a good thing it was, because a sellout crowd of 77,000 jammed into the stadium to see the great Red Grange. Red didn't disappoint, intercepting a pass as the Bears managed to beat the Giants 19–7.

While the Bears were in New York, Pyle opened the doors to all comers to sign Grange to endorsements. Pyle and Grange collected money for endorsing hats, shoes, toys, and soft drinks, but Pyle was upset because he had to turn down a tobacco company since Red didn't smoke. Nevertheless, there certainly was plenty of money to be made from Grange's name and image. He was responsible for the Bears landing on the front page of sports sections throughout the country, and now he was reaping the benefits.

After New York, it was on to the nation's capital to play Washington on December 8. Grange managed to gain only six yards, but the Bears blanked their opponent 19–0. The next day, the Bears traveled to Providence to play the Providence Steamrollers. The Steamrollers won a hard-fought game 9–6 as they limited Grange, who hurt his arm, to 18 yards.

The Bears had played a grueling seven games in less than 15 days. They had 18 players suit up for the Grange tour, and each player wanted to play both on offense and defense. They were physically beat up, but they nevertheless proceeded to Pittsburgh to take on the Steelers.

By the time they got to Pittsburgh, the Bears had only 10 players who were able to take the field. During the game, Grandpa played quarterback. George Trafton and Ed Healey were both so bruised they could hardly walk. When the referee insisted they put an 11th man on the field, Grandpa asked one of the referees to play!

Grange was dealing with some injuries himself. He managed just three yards and one pass reception while the Steelers whipped the Bears 24–0.

After the game, the team headed back to Chicago. Their train stopped in Elkhart, Indiana, where Trafton and Healey, who were great buddies, got off to grab a hamburger. While they were eating their burgers, Healey noticed the train was beginning to pull out, so he yelled, "George, the train's moving!"

Healey ran out of the luncheonette, hurried across the tracks, grabbed hold of the hand rail on the last car, and swung himself aboard. But Trafton was too sore to sprint and never made the train. He stood out on the cold platform without his overcoat, trying to get someone's attention to stop the train, but it went on to Chicago.

All told, the Bears had played 10 games in 18 days. They were exhausted, mentally and physically, but they pushed forward. They played Detroit on December 12 and lost 21–0. Grange wasn't able to play, and since there were only 6,000 people in attendance, each fan received a refund. The team arrived home to host the Giants on December 13. They drew 18,000 people and the Giants won 9–0 as Grange sat out again.

Even though the Bears had suffered a rash of injuries and were physically spent, Pyle had nonetheless been busy promoting. He lined up a nine-game exhibition tour that was to open in Coral Gables, Florida, on Christmas Day. The team arrived in Coral Gables several days early, and Grandpa was dismayed to find that the site for the game was nothing but an open field. They were certain that the game, which guaranteed the Bears $25,000, would be canceled. However, two days before the game, several hundred carpenters went to work around the clock and erected a 30,000-seat stadium made entirely of wood.

The promoter of the game priced tickets anywhere from 50¢ to $18. However, only 8,000 showed up for the game between the Bears and the Florida Collegians, which the Bears won 7–3. Red scored the Bears' only touchdown and averaged 10 yards per carry.

Then on New Year's Day 1926, the Bears played in Florida and defeated the Tampa Cardinals 17–3 as Grange ran for 135 yards and scored two touchdowns (Jim Thorpe happened to be playing for Tampa that day). The next day the Bears played at Jacksonville and beat the Jacksonville Stars 19–6. That day, fullback Ernie Nevers, a future member of the Pro Football Hall of Fame, made his debut with Jacksonville.

The team then traveled to New Orleans, and on January 10 the Bears beat the New Orleans Stars 14–0. Grange ran for 136 yards on 16 carries and scored a touchdown. Six days later, the team was playing in the Los Angeles Coliseum against the Los Angeles Tigers. Grange found the end zone twice as the Bears marched to a 17–7 victory in front of a whopping 75,000 people.

The Bears certainly became quite familiar with the state of California as they went from Los Angeles down to San Diego, then back up to San Francisco. In San Diego, the Bears posted a 14–0 victory over the California Stars, but dropped a 14–9 game to the California Tigers in the City by the Bay.

Oregon was the Bears' next stop on January 30. There, they throttled the Portland Longshoremen 60–3, with Grange scoring twice. The final game of their tour took place in Seattle, and the Bears ended the trip in convincing fashion by whipping the Washington All-Stars 34–0, as Grange ran for 99 yards and two scores.

The tour proved to be successful beyond Pyle's grandest expectations. Grange took home about $125,000, while the tour helped the Bears net approximately $100,000. It marked the Bears' first financially successful season.

Not everyone was celebrating the Bears' success, however. Illinois head football coach Bob Zuppke and George Huff, the school's athletics director, came to Chicago for a Big Ten meeting and stopped by Grandpa's office. Grandpa realized that signing Grange could lead to other professional teams grabbing college stars during the season. Many collegiate coaches were not fond of professional football, and after talking to Zuppke and Huff Grandpa vowed he would do everything he could to prevent this practice in the future.

In February 1926, NFL officials met and adopted what became known as the Red Grange Resolution. This rule stated that no college football player would be eligible to play in the NFL until his class had graduated. It would prove to be beneficial to college football and certainly to the professional ranks, but more importantly, it put an emphasis on young men in college earning their degrees.

The league also decided to raise Joe Carr's salary to $6,500 a year, and league franchises were now valued at $2,500. Carr also laid down the law when he fined the Milwaukee Badgers $500, and gave the Milwaukee owner 90 days to dispose of his assets and have the team leave the league, after four high school boys played for the Badgers in a game against the Cardinals. The Cardinals, meanwhile, were fined $1,000 and put on probation for a year.

Early in the year, the Maroons, a team from Pottsville, Pennsylvania, had been charged with encroaching on another team's territory when they played a game against a team that wasn't a member of the league. Pottsville was slapped with a $500 fine for this incident and had to forfeit its franchise. However, the franchise was reinstated when the NFL held its annual league meeting in June.

During that June meeting, a disagreement erupted between Pyle, the Bears, and the NFL. Not content with the deal he had made with the Bears, Pyle demanded one-third of the Bears' stock now that Grange was playing for the team. Grandpa and Dutch refused. Pyle then wanted to start his own football team in New York, call it the Yankees, and have them play in Yankee Stadium. The team would directly rival the Giants, so Giants owner Tim Mara blocked him from doing so.

Pyle, however, was not about to take "no" for an answer. So he started the American Football League with nine teams: the Boston Bulldogs, Brooklyn Horsemen, Chicago Bulls, Cleveland Panthers, Los Angeles Wildcats, Newark Bears, New York Yankees, Philadelphia Quakers, and Rock Island Independents (Rock Island was a charter member of the NFL but jumped to the new league).

The AFL proved to be the first major challenge to the NFL. It would compete with the NFL for talent and fans, and go head-to-head with it in five different cities: Brooklyn, Chicago, Cleveland, Philadelphia, and, of course, New York. Big Bill Edwards, a former Princeton athlete, became the league's president. Pyle led the New York franchise and took Red Grange with him. At about the same time, Joey Sternaman—Dutch's younger brother who quarterbacked the Bears and was their leading scorer in 1925—left the Bears to become the Bulls' new owner and coach. Within a short period of time, the Bears had lost two of their most popular players. The Bulls leased Comiskey Park, which forced the Chicago Cardinals into much smaller Normal Park.

In the midst of all the wheeling and dealing going on within the American Football League, Grandpa was about to land a player he had coveted for a long time. He learned that Paddy Driscoll was considering jumping to the Bulls. When the Cardinals could not match the offer Driscoll received from the Bulls, they sold him to the Bears for $3,500. Grandpa, in turn, gave Driscoll a $10,000 contract.

Driscoll paid dividends right from the get-go. Three games into the 1926 season, Driscoll not only kicked a field goal but also threw a 50-yard touchdown pass as the team beat the Detroit Panthers 10–7. The next week, Paddy scored the game's only touchdown and kicked the extra point to lead the Bears to a 7–0 victory over the Giants.

The Bears ended up playing the Chicago Cardinals three times that season. Their first meeting took place at Normal Park, and 12,000 fans turned out to see Paddy play against his old team. But Red Grange and the New York Yankees happened to be in town the same day to play the Bulls, and that matchup drew 20,000 to Comiskey Park.

Driscoll put on a one-man show that day. He scored a touchdown, booted three field goals, and added an extra point en route to the Bears' 16–0 win over the Cardinals. Grandpa received a blow to the head during the second quarter and was taken to the locker room. The hit threw Grandpa for a loop; Andy Lotshaw, the team trainer, later said

Paddy Driscoll quarterbacked the Bears from 1926 to 1929, coached them in 1956 and 1957, and was inducted into the Pro Football Hall of Fame in 1965.

Grandpa had asked him who they were playing. When Lotshaw replied, "the Cardinals," Grandpa said, "Then this must be Thanksgiving Day." Oscar Knop, the Bears' fullback, did not suit up for the Cardinals game because he was recovering from some earlier injuries. But when Grandpa saw Oscar sitting in street clothes, Grandpa told him to get into uniform and out on the field. After hearing that, Lotshaw decided Grandpa was too punchy and better not play the second half.

This game also was noteworthy because the Bears hired a band to perform at halftime and during timeouts, marking the first time a professional team had used musical entertainment.

On Armistice Day (November 11), the Bears played the Cardinals again at Soldier Field in what was billed as a benefit for Rosary College.

Driscoll threw a 60-yard touchdown strike to Duke Hanny and also kicked a field goal to lead the Bears to a 10–0 win. On Thanksgiving Day, the Bears and the Cardinals played to a scoreless tie, but by that time the Bears had recorded 10 wins for the season after beating the Green Bay Packers the weekend before.

In the season's final game, the Bears were matched up against the Frankford Yellow Jackets. If the Bears could beat the Yellow Jackets, they would be league champions. But Grandpa's old friend Guy Chamberlin, who was coaching the Yellow Jackets at that time, decided to play in this game, and he had a great day at the Bears' expense. The Bears scored first, but Chamberlin broke through and blocked Driscoll's extra-point attempt. Later, Driscoll tried a field goal from the 24-yard line, but again Chamberlin blocked it. The Bears were still leading 6–0 with two minutes left, but the Yellow Jackets scored, added the point-after, and won the championship by a final score of 7–6. If they had only defeated the Yellow Jackets, the Bears would have been the champions with a sparkling 13–0–3 record.

At season's end, the Bears showed a profit of $1,271.62, but many NFL clubs were in sad shape financially. The manager of the NFL's Los Angeles Buccaneers, Jack McDonough, went so far as to say, "Professional football has breathed its last. It has failed to strike the popular fancy."

The AFL was in even worse shape. Some AFL clubs folded before the end of its season, and by the end of the year, only the New York Yankees, Philadelphia Quakers, Chicago Bulls, and Rock Island Independents were still playing. The league itself ended up folding after its first season.

With the rival league now out of the picture, the NFL made a healthy recovery in 1927. The league recognized the fact that Red Grange was very important to the game, so when Pyle applied for a franchise this time around, he was granted one, and the Yankees joined the NFL.

The 1927 Bears enjoyed a very good year, finishing in third place behind the Giants and Packers with a 9–3–2 record. Their profits had increased to $1,964.05, which included a profit on programs of $2,262.43. The Bears started the 1927 campaign with a 9–0 victory over the Cardinals. Then the Bears beat Green Bay 7–6. In the third game of the year, Grange returned to Wrigley Field as a member of the Yankees to play the Bears. (The name of the field had changed from Cubs Park to Wrigley Field after 1926.) Around 30,000 packed into the park, but it turned out to be a sad day for Grange.

The Bears won the game 12–0, but in the final minutes, Grange suffered a serious knee injury. Grange had George Trafton covering him as he went out for a pass. Just as Grange reached for the ball, Trafton fell on him. When both players went down, Grange's cleats got caught in the turf.

Grange missed the next four games and wasn't able to play much the rest of the year. He also ended up missing all of 1928. The Bears reacquired Grange prior to the 1929 season, but it was apparent that the knee injury had robbed "the Galloping Ghost"—a nickname given to him by *Chicago American* sportswriter Warren Brown—of his sensational ability to make cuts. He was no longer football's greatest and most exciting runner.

Overall, 1928 proved to be an average year for the Bears. The team dipped to 7–5–1 and finished toward the middle of the pack in the NFL, which contracted from 12 teams to 10. (The Duluth Eskimos and Buffalo Bisons, who finished 1927 second-to-last and last, respectively, dropped out of the league.) Grandpa was still coaching and playing, as well as handling all of the Bears' front office duties.

In 1929, the aforementioned Galloping Ghost, along with quarterback Joey Sternaman, returned to the Bears, but they didn't help the team's fortunes that year. Despite winning four of its first six games, the club finished a disappointing 4–9–2. Dutch and Grandpa were getting up there in years, as far as playing football, and realized the team needed an infusion of new blood. They started right at the top, and approached

Bronko Nagurski was a charter member of the Pro Football Hall of Fame.

Ralph Jones—Grandpa's freshman football coach at Illinois who was the athletics director at Lake Forest Academy at the time—about taking over as head coach. They thought highly of him, so much so that they offered him $10,000 a year—a substantial sum, considering the nation had just experienced the stock-market crash of 1929 and was on the verge of the Great Depression.

Jones made a promise to Grandpa and Dutch—"I'll give you the championship in three years"—as he signed his contract. At that time, Dutch and Grandpa issued a statement indicating their front office duties had taken away from their coaching. Thus, they thought it would be best for the team to have a coach who would be fully devoted to the team.

Grandpa celebrated his 34th birthday and realized it was time for him to retire from playing. Now he would have more time to devote to Min and their two growing children: Virginia, my mother, who was born in 1923; and George Jr., my uncle, who was born in 1925. The year George Jr. was born, Grandpa also had become an owner of the Chicago Bruins of the American Basketball League, but only after he had persuaded Joe Carr, the NFL president, to serve as president of the ABL.

In addition, Grandpa got into real estate with a firm called Halas and Kraft. He also was part owner of a retail jewelry store, a sporting goods store, and a laundry business.

Paddy Driscoll decided to retire after the 1929 season, leaving the Bears with some big shoes to fill offensively. However, Grandpa was able to acquire a handful of players during the off-season who would make a big impact over the next few years—including the great Bronislau "Bronko" Nagurski, who later would be inducted into the Pro Football Hall of Fame. Nagurski, whom *Sports Illustrated* would name one of the three greatest athletes in Minnesota state history (Kevin McHale and Dave Winfield being the others), had played both tackle and fullback at the University of Minnesota, earning All-America honors at each position.

The Bears also signed Carl Brumbaugh, who would become one of the all-time great Bears, out of the University of Florida. Brumbaugh played halfback at Florida, but with a trio of pretty fine halfbacks already on the roster—notably Red Grange, Larry Walquist, and Bill Senn—he decided to try out for quarterback. Good thing he did because Joey Sternaman, the team's regular quarterback, got hurt early in the season, so Brumbaugh was able to take over. Ralph Jones also inherited George Trafton, Luke Johnsos at end, fullback Walter Holmer, and one of the greatest tackles Grandpa had ever seen, Roy "Link" Lyman, another future Hall of Famer.

When Dutch and Grandpa played football at Illinois, head coach Bob Zuppke utilized the T formation offense. But Grandpa long believed that the true architect of the T formation with a man in motion was Ralph Jones. Jones' version of the T put running backs in a perfect position for straight-ahead plunges or quick hitters, particularly between the tackles.

However, Jones reworked the T by splitting the ends two yards from the tackles, and by spacing the halfbacks even wider so that they lined up behind the tackles. Then he added his master stroke: he put one of the halfbacks in motion. As the quarterback started calling signals, the halfback started laterally toward the sideline. By the time the center snapped the ball, the in-motion halfback had gotten far out in the flank. The halfback then would either block an opposing defender or move into the defensive backfield as a pass receiver. Jones' imaginative use of the T really put the heat on opposing defenses.

When Jones and the Bears started the 1930 season, they began experimenting with the T formation. In early November, they faced the Green Bay Packers for the second time, hoping to avenge a 7–0 loss to the Packers back in September. Normally, Red Grange would go in motion to his right, but the Packers shifted a defender to cover him. To counter this, Grange suggested that he first start out to the right, then reverse his position and go toward the left sideline. Grange believed this might confuse the Packers, and it did. When he went in motion to the left, a Green Bay linebacker followed him. This left an opening up the middle, and Nagurski was able to pound out long yardage every time the linebacker followed Grange to the left.

Packers defensive backs were also keeping tabs on Grange in motion, which opened things up for Johnsos at end. This left the Packers thoroughly confused, and left Johnsos wide open to catch passes from Brumbaugh.

However, the Packers were a formidable team. They were unbeaten in 21 consecutive contests going into the game, and the 22,000 people who had assembled at Wrigley Field to watch the game that day knew they were tough. The Packers held a 13–6 lead going into the final two minutes, but Nagurski took the ball and tore up the middle of the line, carrying would-be tacklers with him, to set up a Walquist touchdown. The Bears trailed by only one point, and all Walter Holmer had to do was kick the extra point. But he missed it, and the Bears lost 13–12.

The Bears' failure to tie the game may have cost them the championship. They ended up with a 9–4–1 record, compared to the Packers' 10–3–1 mark. The two teams met for a third time in early December, and the Bears had no trouble beating them 21–0 as the T formation worked to perfection. The November game marked the Bears debut of All-American fullback "Jumping Joe" Savoldi. Savoldi was forced to leave the University of Notre Dame prior to his graduation because he got married. When he left school, Grandpa believed that it was okay to sign him because he was no longer a college student. Although Joe Carr sided with Grandpa on this matter, Grandpa nevertheless urged Carr to fine the Bears $1,000 because Grandpa wanted to make sure no one thought he was violating the league rule against signing players whose class had not yet graduated. The Bears weren't able to pay the $1,000 immediately, but they did pay it off in installments. Savoldi scored the team's only touchdown when the Bears beat the Cardinals on Thanksgiving Day.

In mid-December, just after the season ended, the Bears went up against the Cardinals once again, this time in an exhibition game. With the country now in the grips of the Great Depression, the governor of Illinois, Louis Emerson, asked the Bears to assist the Illinois Unemployment Relief Fund by playing the Cardinals indoors at Chicago Stadium. The stadium held 20,000, but the teams were forced to play on an 80-yard field that consisted of several inches of dirt spread out on the floor. The Bears nipped the Cardinals 9–7.

Through the years, Grandpa always had some interesting relationships with officials who worked Bears games. One of Grandpa's favorites, Bobby Cahn, officiated the exhibition game at Chicago Stadium. Cahn stood only 5'2" and weighed around 140 pounds. But he was ferocious controlling the game and didn't hesitate to tell off a massive lineman or anyone else on the field. He would dive into a pile and come up with the ball; his word was the law.

At one point during the exhibition game, he called a penalty on the Bears. Grandpa, who was sitting on the bench next to Ralph Jones, jumped up and said, "Cahn, you stink." Cahn looked over at Grandpa very calmly, walked off an additional 15 yards, and yelled, "Halas, how do I smell from here?"

The 1930 Chicago Bears completely reversed their fortunes from the previous year, and Jones had made an auspicious debut as a head coach in the National Football League. Although the Bears had announced Jones would be paid $10,000 a year when they signed him, he actually received only $7,500.

Things were very tough financially in 1930, so Grandpa and Dutch Sternaman decided not to take salaries. Sternaman relied on his work at the gas station, as well as some oil interests that he had developed, to see him through financially. Meanwhile, Grandpa lived off all his aforementioned business ventures. He also had an interest in a development at Lake Geneva, Wisconsin, which encompassed a golf course and lodge—a lodge that Gene Tunney used as his training site for his fight with Jack Dempsey at Soldier Field in 1929.

Even though the team drew well in 1930, the Bears showed a loss of $490.52. The total payroll for players that season was $53,369.83. Nagurski turned out to be their highest-paid player at $5,000, while Savoldi, with his bonus and salary, took home $4,000.

Grandpa kept his head above water by giving IOU notes to the players he owed money. He gave an IOU of $1,000 to Ralph Jones, while Savoldi, Holmer, Nagurski, and guard Dan McMullen each received IOUs of $500. By giving IOUs, the Bears showed a book profit of $1,695.93 at the end of the 1930, and Grandpa was able to pay $100 to Nagurski and $200 to McMullen.

As 1931 dawned, a meeting was arranged between Grandpa and Dr. David Jones, the owner of the Cardinals. They decided to divide the Chicago area between the two competing teams so that each would fare better financially. The Cardinals would retain their territory south of Madison Street, and the Bears would concentrate on all territory north of Madison Street. Soldier Field would remain neutral territory.

The 1931 Bears put together a season similar to 1930. They finished 8–5, and once again placed third in the league behind Green Bay and Portsmouth. One of the year's highlights came in the person of another Grange—Red's brother, Garland, who scored a game-winning touchdown after catching a pass from Brumbaugh with 22 seconds remaining as the Bears defeated the Giants 12–6 in the eighth game of the season. Garland initially joined the Bears as a favor to Red. He played well for the Bears from 1929 through 1931, but he always lived in Red's shadow. Even when he scored the winning touchdown versus the Giants, the headlines in the newspapers read, "Red Grange's Brother Beats Giants on Pass."

The team welcomed a handful of new players who would make important contributions that season. The most notable newcomer was Keith Molesworth, an explosive running back at Monmouth (Illinois) College who eventually became Brumbaugh's backup at quarterback. Molesworth, who had also played shortstop for Baltimore in the International League, lined up as a safety in punting situations for the Bears. He would make running catches in much the same way a center fielder would in baseball. A very dangerous runner who also turned out to be a good punter and receiver, he'd catch the ball on a dead run so that he had a full head of steam to get past tacklers. After Molesworth retired from football, he went on to become a backfield coach at the Naval Academy for many years.

Nagurski also recommended one of his teammates at Minnesota, Herb Joesting, a future College Football Hall of Fame member who backed up Nagurski at fullback. In addition to Molesworth and Joesting, the Bears added two linemen from the University of Illinois, Ed Kawal and Lloyd Burdick. They also signed Southern California All-American offensive tackle Jesse Hibbs, who was born in downstate Normal, Illinois, and found a sleeper in the person of Art Bramhall, a very fast halfback who happened to be playing on the Chicago Bruins basketball team that Grandpa owned.

Signing new players wasn't at the top of Grandpa's to-do list prior to the 1931 season, however. Dutch Sternaman was experiencing financial difficulties, and he wanted Grandpa to buy him out of his 50 percent share of the Bears, which totaled $38,000. Grandpa agreed to buy Dutch out because he wanted to take full control of the team, but where in the world was he going to get $38,000, especially in the middle of a depression? What particularly worried Grandpa about the buyout was that if he couldn't raise the money, he would lose everything he had already invested in the team.

Dutch drew up a deal through his lawyer, which required Grandpa to pay $25,000 in cash. Another $6,000 was due by January 25, 1932, and the final $7,000 by July 31, 1932.

Despite the odds, Grandpa went to work. He had already tapped his children's savings accounts ($600 each) and compiled a list of people he could approach for money.

Fortunately, several individuals were able to loan Grandpa some money: Jim McMillen, who was with the Bears; Grandpa's dear friend Charlie Bidwill, vice president of the Bears who later owned the Chicago Cardinals; Ralph Brizzolara, a close friend of Grandpa's since high school; and even George Trafton's mother.

Grandpa paid Dutch $25,000 in July, but was still $13,000 short of reaching the sum needed to take control of the team. If Grandpa failed to raise the final $13,000, the stock would go back to Dutch, according to the deal. He went back to the drawing board and made another list of people he could contact. He even thought about contacting Frank Zambrino, who had worked with C.C. Pyle in the Red Grange negotiations.

A year passed. July 31, 1932, arrived, and despite his best efforts, Grandpa remained $5,000 short. Under the agreement, Dutch assumed control of the stock. Dutch's lawyer then sent Grandpa a letter, stating that Dutch's stock would go up for public auction on August 9.

Desperation set in. Grandpa needed the $5,000 by noon of August 9 or he would lose control of the Bears. At 11:00 that morning, the phone rang. C.K. Anderson—president of the First National Bank of Antioch, Illinois, who had worked with Grandpa on the Lake Petite development and hosting Gene Tunney before his fight with Jack Dempsey—was on the other end of the line. He agreed to lend Grandpa the money, and not a moment too soon. Grandpa had about 30 minutes. He raced over to Dutch's lawyer's office and handed him the check just 10 minutes before noon! Grandpa gained control of his beloved team.

No Raise for Ookie

On Saturday, November 5, 1932, Charles "Ookie" Miller—a center and linebacker who played for the Bears during the 1930s—saw New York City for the first time in his life. Ookie went to the Cotton Club to see Cab Calloway the night before the Bears played the Giants. When Ookie returned to his room, there was a note on his door:

"Ookie, when you get in, come see me. George."

When they met, Grandpa asked Ookie point-blank, "Hey, Ookie, did you have a good time last night?"

Ookie tried to explain to Grandpa that it was his first trip to New York. Grandpa, however, didn't appreciate that Ookie had gone out for a night on the town.

"Don't worry about it, kid," Grandpa said. "It will only cost you $100."

Ookie didn't like getting the fine, and thought he would take a stand. He told his teammates he wouldn't play if it was going to cost him $100. But one teammate told Ookie not to worry about it; that player had a similar experience with Grandpa, and the fine was rescinded after he played a good game. So he advised Ookie to just play a good game against New York.

Ookie did play and played well, as the Bears won 28–8. After the game, Grandpa approached Miller and said, "Ookie, I think I'll fine you $100 every game—you play better." Miller, however, did not get a refund, much to his surprise.

After the season, Grandpa called Ookie in for a meeting to discuss a contract for 1933. Ookie had played 60 minutes in most games, so he was pretty confident he could get a raise.

Grandpa had other ideas, however, and used some reverse psychology.

"Gee, kid, you had a great season, and '33 should be better, but we lost money in '32," Grandpa told Ookie. "I was going to cut everyone's salary, but you had such a great year, I'll keep your salary the same as last year and we'll consider this a raise."

Ookie didn't get a raise, but he left his meeting with Grandpa feeling as if he had.

Finally, Grandpa could concentrate on football again. He added two players who would end up contributing immediately to the Bears in 1932. Bill Hewitt, a University of Michigan star who refused to wear a helmet, was probably one of the greatest ends to ever play the game. He would end up being named to the NFL's All-Decade Team in the 1930s, as well as to the Pro Football Hall of Fame. The Bears also signed a big, strong youngster from Milwaukee, John Doehring, who had never played college football. His Bears teammates immediately pinned the nickname of "Bull" on Doehring, who played fullback.

Grandpa couldn't believe it when he saw what Bull could do with a football. Despite being a running back, Doehring, who was left-handed, could throw forward passes behind his back, if he wanted to.

Doehring was also blessed with a peculiar personality. For example, the Bears were scheduled to play against the Boston Braves in the sixth week of the season, but when they started to dress for the game, Doehring was nowhere to be found. After the game, he strolled into the clubhouse in street clothes and started to get undressed.

One of the players asked, "Why are you getting undressed now?"

Bull replied, "I think I'll take a shower."

"Where were you during the game?"

"In the stands watching the game."

"But you were supposed to play the game."

Bull said, "I know, but I got to thinking on my way over to the park that maybe my mother didn't want me to play professional football."

Well, his teammates straightened Doehring out pretty quickly, and Bull was in uniform for the Bears' game against Portsmouth on November 27. It was then that Bull—who many Bears players believed could throw a ball 90 yards—exhibited his great throwing arm. During one play, he took a lateral from Brumbaugh, hesitated for a moment, then threw a pass 65 yards in the air to Luke Johnsos, who had gotten behind a Portsmouth safety. Johnsos took it the rest of the way for a touchdown.

In what would be Ralph Jones' final year as head coach, the Bears stood on top of the NFL standings with a 7–1–6 record. Some of the players who contributed mightily that season included Paul "Tiny" Engebretsen, a guard out of Northwestern; Johnny Sisk, a tough halfback from Marquette; Charles "Ookie" Miller, a lineman from Purdue who earned his nickname because of his love for cookies; and Joe Kopcha out of Chattanooga. Kopcha, an All-Pro offensive guard for three consecutive years, would later go on to medical school and become renowned as an obstetrician.

The season started out strangely. The Bears played their first three opponents to scoreless ties, then suffered a 2–0 loss to Green Bay in their fourth game. But from that point on, their offense picked up, their defense remained formidable, and they went 7–0–3 the rest of the way. The Bears finished the regular season with a 9–0 win over the Packers, but the game was played under extremely difficult conditions. Snow had been falling for weeks in Chicago, and temperatures were constantly below zero. Because of the weather, the playoff game was moved indoors to Chicago Stadium. As they did two years before against the Cardinals, the Bears had to play on a field consisting of six inches of dirt that measured 80 yards long and 40 yards wide. The goal posts were moved from the back of the end zones to the goal lines. And to compensate for the shorter field, anytime each offensive team crossed midfield, the ball was automatically moved back to the 20-yard line.

The Bears' record earned them a spot in the NFL Championship Game against the Portsmouth Spartans—the first playoff game ever held by the NFL. Earlier in the year, the Bears and Portsmouth met twice, with the games ending in ties of 13–13 and 7–7.

The Bears caught a lucky break right at the start of the championship game when they learned that Dutch Clark, Portsmouth's outstanding quarterback, couldn't play because he was coaching the Colorado College basketball team. The school didn't consider the NFL Championship Game important enough to allow him take part in it.

Each team displayed stingy defense, and the game remained scoreless through the first three quarters. However, Dick Nesbitt, playing halfback for the Bears on defense, intercepted a pass and ran the ball back to the Portsmouth 7-yard line. Portsmouth knew what was coming: the Bears gave the ball to Nagurski, and he bulled up the middle for six yards to put the Bears at the 1-yard line. Portsmouth assumed the Bears would give the ball to Nagurski again, and so they tightened up in the middle. Nagurski ran the ball twice, but Portsmouth stopped him both times.

Anticipating that Nagurski would again try to run up the gut, the Spartans closed up the middle once more. This time, however, the Bears pulled off a play that would in many ways change all of football. Nagurski started running up the middle, but when he got to the line of scrimmage, he stopped and backpedalled. He was looking for Red Grange, who had cut around the end and was weaving into the end zone. When Nagurski saw Grange, he lobbed a pass to Grange for the touchdown.

Potsy Clark, head coach of the Spartans, jumped up and down, screaming and hollering that the play was illegal. He insisted that Nagurski was not the required five yards behind the line of scrimmage when he threw the pass to Grange; he was only two yards back. However, the officials allowed the touchdown to stand. The Bears kicked the point-after, and later scored a safety to win the game 9–0 and capture their first NFL championship. The next day, newspapers and the fans debated whether or not Nagurski was actually five yards behind the line of scrimmage when he threw the pass.

At that time, many NFL games were either low-scoring or ended in a tie. Grandpa knew that the game had to be opened up if the NFL was to become more appealing to the fans who were footing the bill. The play involving Nagurski and Grange made Grandpa realize that the NFL could achieve the desired result of opening up the game if one could pass from anywhere behind the line of scrimmage.

Even though the Bears wrapped up their first NFL title in 1932, it turned out to be a bad year financially; they lost $18,000 and couldn't meet their expenses. Grandpa couldn't ask any of the banks around the area to lend him money because they didn't have any money to lend. The future of the Bears and of professional football itself was hanging in the balance.

Chapter 6

RETURN TO COACHING

D espite the team's financial woes and the country wallowing in the depths of the worst economic depression in its history, the 1933 season would prove to be one of the most important years not only for the Bears, but for the NFL as well.

In February of that year, the league held its annual meeting at the Fort Pitt Hotel in Pittsburgh. Under the guidance of strong leaders such as my grandfather, Curly Lambeau of Green Bay, Tim Mara of the New York Giants, and George Preston Marshall of the Boston Redskins, the league passed three rules that proved vital to the future of professional football. One of the rules made hash marks a permanent part of the field. Hash marks—small lines that mark each yard on the field between 5-yard lines—were added 10 yards in from each sideline; every play would begin with the ball placed either on one of the hash marks or between them. Another important rule change saw the goal posts moved from the back of the end zone to the goal line in order to increase the number of field goals, which the league hoped would reduce the number of tied games.

The controversial play involving Bronko Nagurski's pass behind the line of scrimmage during the 1932 title game between the Bears and Portsmouth led to a third important rule change. Marshall made a motion, which Grandpa seconded, to enact a rule that would permit a forward pass to be thrown from anywhere behind the line of scrimmage, rather than a passer having to be at least five yards behind the line of scrimmage. This turned out to be a very important rule change because it made the game faster and much more exciting for the fans.

Marshall also was instrumental in the decision to split NFL teams into two divisions that year—the Eastern Division and the Western Division—with the winners of each division playing for the NFL championship at the end of the year. In addition, he wanted to abolish the huddle; he wanted to see any team that went into a huddle punished by charging them with a timeout. But poor George just smiled and had to let his "no huddle" rule go by the wayside because no one else at the meeting seconded the proposal.

Although the steps taken by the NFL at its February meeting were important because of their effect on the game, the league also held a meeting in early July at the Blackstone Hotel in Chicago that was just as important. At this meeting, the league received a handful of applications for membership. The league allowed a group in Cincinnati to join the NFL; the team was called the Cincinnati Reds, after the city's Major League Baseball team. It also allowed Art Rooney, who would become an NFL legend, to start a franchise in Pittsburgh and call the team the Pirates (later, of course, it would change its name to the Steelers).

Lud Wray applied for membership with a franchise to replace the Frankford Yellow Jackets. The franchise would be based in Philadelphia and be known as the Eagles—a team Wray also coached. However, the Eagles were allowed into the league only after agreeing to pay 25 percent of liens that were held by Green Bay, the Bears, and the Giants.

Times were tough financially, so the league took an additional step in order to bring in more money. Mara made a motion, seconded by Charlie Bidwill (who had taken over the Chicago Cardinals) and unanimously approved, that upped the application fee for future franchises to $10,000 as long as 10 or more clubs were in the NFL.

Other small provisions were enacted during the July meeting as well. All clubs had to have at least two new official league balls ready for use prior to each game. The Spalding J-5 unlined ball was adopted as the official ball of the National Football League in 1933.

The league also assigned team colors and passed provisions for neatness of appearance by players on both teams. Additionally, each club was required to have a football timing watch and pistol with blank cartridges for use by the officials during home games.

Teams spent a great deal of time scheduling games, so the league decided to allow its president, Joe Carr, to oversee forming a schedule. Eventually, the NFL formed a committee whose goal was to develop a schedule for presentation at the NFL meeting the following year.

One of the first tasks Grandpa faced going into the 1933 season was finding a new head coach. Ralph Jones decided he had enough of pro football after the Bears won the championship in 1932, and he retired to become the athletics director at Lake Forest College.

Grandpa sifted through many applications, both formal and informal. He fielded applications from coaches who were already under contract at top colleges and universities, high school coaches, and former players, all of whom wanted to give it a go with the Bears in 1933. This was quite a switch from just a few years ago when college coaches looked down their noses at the pros.

However, it became more apparent to Grandpa that he wanted a coach who was a pupil of Jones and Bob Zuppke—the latter also had played for the Bears and had some coaching experience. Who would that candidate be? None of the above!

Prior to the start of the season, the announcement was made that George Halas would return to coach the Chicago Bears for one year only. During Jones' tenure, Grandpa studied every move he made, especially Jones' development of the T formation. He believed he could put the knowledge he gained watching Jones to work for the Bears.

Absorb-ine Some Costs

Ookie Miller had a charley horse and Bronko Nagurski was nursing a sore hip prior to the Bears' October 8, 1933, game in Brooklyn against the Dodgers. When the team arrived in Brooklyn, Grandpa arranged for boxing great Jack Dempsey's trainer to work on Bronko and Ookie before the game. In addition to bringing in Dempsey's trainer, Grandpa purchased a bottle of Absorbine Jr. to use on their injuries.

The next day, the Bears won 10–0. On the train ride back to Chicago, Grandpa paid Ookie his game salary in cash, as was customary in those days. But Ookie noticed Grandpa had not paid him his entire salary for that game.

"George, you are a dollar short," Ookie told Grandpa.

"That's for the bottle of Absorbine Jr.," Grandpa replied.

Ookie said, "Yeah, but it was also used on Bronk."

"Yeah," Grandpa noted, "but you kept the bottle!"

The Bears' roster at that time looked good to Grandpa. Nagurski, Red Grange, and Brumbaugh—considered the smartest quarterback in the NFL at that time—remained entrenched in the team's backfield, while Bill Hewitt and Luke Johnsos returned at the ends. Grandpa and the Bears also welcomed several new players who were destined for NFL stardom: offensive linemen Ray Richards, Joe Zeller, rookie George Musso—a Millikin University (Decatur, Illinois) product who played 12 seasons with the Bears and once lined up opposite future presidents Gerald Ford and Ronald Reagan—and halfback/place-kicker Jack Manders, who would earn the nickname "Automatic Jack."

Another star rookie, Gene Ronzani, could play fullback, halfback, and quarterback, as well as punt. Ronzani, who had a great football mind, later went into coaching as an assistant and then became head coach at Green Bay. At one time in Bears history, Ronzani operated their farm club at Newark (the Newark Bears). During World War II,

My grandfather coached the Staleys/Bears to 318 regular-season wins during his career.

he came back to play quarterback for the Bears when they were hard-pressed for personnel.

The team also brought back Link Lyman, an outstanding tackle who had retired from football in 1932. When he returned in 1933, he was in his thirties, making him one of the old men on the squad. However, he could still move fast for a man weighing 250 pounds. Grandpa could always count on him to be the first man downfield on punts while continuing to be a fixture at tackle. Lyman served as a father figure to many of the younger players, and he was the life of the party on road trips.

The Century of Progress exposition was being held in Chicago that year in order to breathe life into the economy. As part of the publicity buildup for this exposition, the Bears held training camp in South Bend in order to enhance publicity for an exhibition game they were going to have with the Notre Dame All-Stars, then coached by Heartley William "Hunk" Anderson. The Bears and Notre Dame played in the mud at Soldier Field, with the Bears winning 14–0.

Interestingly, Grandpa also discovered end Bill Karr around the time of the exhibition game. Karr, a fantastic three-sport athlete at the University of West Virginia where he had majored in chemistry, fully expected to go on and earn his master's degree, then become a chemistry teacher. He wasn't overwhelmed when the Bears invited him to their tryout, but he did want to see the Century of Progress, so he came to Chicago. When he ran out of money, he reported to the Bears.

Karr didn't impress the Bears during early practice sessions. As a second-string end, he was expected to stop Ronzani on sweeps, but he had to contend with the blocking of Nagurski first. Karr never made a tackle. The Bears were about to let him go, but one day, Tarz Taylor, a former Bears player, stopped to watch practice.

Taylor studied Karr, then approached Grandpa later at practice. Taylor said, "I think that boy is sick, or something is wrong with him." Grandpa looked into the situation and discovered Karr was broke. If

Karr ever did get anything to eat, it wasn't much more than a hamburger. When the Bears realized this, Taylor said, "Feed him and he'll make a fine football player." Grandpa gave Bill Karr an advance, and Karr began to eat properly. He then blossomed into one of the Bears' brightest stars.

Hewitt and Johnsos, the Bears' regular ends, took an interest in Karr. Toward the middle of the season, Johnsos broke his leg, which gave Karr a chance to play. From that point on, Karr proved that he was indeed a great football player.

George Musso was another intriguing player. He weighed 260 pounds and played with plenty of desire and speed. But Grandpa already had a plethora of good players in his stable. The Bears were about to make a trip to play Boston and Brooklyn when Grandpa told Musso he was going to release him. Musso, however, pleaded with Grandpa to let him make the trip. Even though Green Bay had offered him a contract, he told Grandpa, "I'll make this trip for half my salary because I don't want to leave the team."

Since Musso was already rooming in an apartment with Nagurski and George Corbin, Grandpa agreed to keep him. They cut his salary from $90 a week to $60 a week. But Musso played such terrific football during the two games out East that Grandpa was happy to forget all about the salary arrangement and reinstated him at $90 per week. Musso became one of the truly great Bears.

The Bears opened up the 1933 season in the new Western Division against the rival Packers in Green Bay. The Bears trailed the entire contest, but managed to rally for two touchdowns in the final two minutes to beat the Packers. My grandma Min was in the stands that day. Convinced that the Bears were going to lose, she started back to the car early for the return trip to Chicago. Just as she got back to the car—surprise!—she got word that the Bears had won.

The Bears went on to register two shutout victories—first a 7–0 win over the Boston Redskins, then a 10–0 whitewash of the Brooklyn

George Musso spent his entire 12-year career with the Bears.

Dodgers at Ebbets Field. The team returned home to Wrigley Field to take on their crosstown rivals, the Cardinals, and ended up defeating them by using the oldest football trick in the book: the famous "sleeper play" that is no longer legal. Brumbaugh called for a running play. When the ball carrier was tackled, Johnsos bent down in front of the bench as if he were tying his shoelace. The Cardinals didn't pay any attention to him; when the ball was snapped, Johnsos streaked down the sideline and Brumbaugh hit him with a pass. There wasn't a Cardinal anywhere near him, and he went in for a touchdown. The Bears beat the Cardinals 12–9 for their fourth straight victory.

One week later, the Bears hosted the Packers, and it turned out to be another memorable matchup. The Bears won this one in the last minute, which proved a point Grandpa often made: it's better to be lucky than good. The Bears blocked a punt and took possession on their own 43-yard line in the game's final minute. The Packers anticipated the Bears would attempt a pass. Instead, they sent Jack Manders up the middle for 27 yards. Three plays later, Manders booted a field goal from 30 yards out to break a 7–7 tie and the Bears won 10–7 as the gun sounded.

Another exciting contest awaited the Bears a week later as they took on the Giants. Unfortunately, the Bears ended up losing Johnsos for the season when he broke his leg attempting to block a punt. But the Bears pulled out a 14–10 victory when Bill Karr, who had replaced Johnsos, scored on an end-around play.

Later that year, Bronko Nagurski turned the tide for the Bears in a game versus Portsmouth when he powered 55 yards up the middle despite six Portsmouth tacklers taking shots at him as he ran. Nothing could stop Bronko that day; in fact, he ran so hard that when he got into the end zone, he attempted to stop but slid headfirst into the concrete wall of one of the Wrigley Field dugouts.

The Bears experienced only one dry spell in 1933. They went on the road and lost a tough game to Boston 10–0, then another to the Giants 3–0. These defeats book-ended a 3–3 tie with the Philadelphia Eagles. The contest against the Eagles turned out to be important from a social standpoint. It marked the first time an athletic event had been held on a Sunday in Philadelphia. Earlier, the Keystone State repealed a "blue law"—laws that enforced moral standards and Sunday as a day of rest—that had been in effect for more than 100 years. Philadelphia residents responded to the repeal of the law, as 17,850 of them came to the Baker Bowl to see the game.

Finally, the Bears closed out their regular season by knocking off the Packers for the third time in 1933, this time 7–6. Grandpa's return to coaching proved successful as the Bears finished 10–2–1 and qualified for the NFL Championship Game by winning the Western Division. They would square off against the Giants, who won the Eastern Division crown, on December 17.

The day before the title game, league representatives met for a third time. This meeting, which took place at the Sherman Hotel in Chicago, was devoted largely to scheduling matters. Scheduling for the 1934 season was on everyone's mind because it factored into gate receipts as well as the obvious concern: winning and losing. So a new scheduling committee, which replaced the one created in 1933, was proposed and unanimously approved. This committee would consist of Carr and four committee members—two from each division.

The next day, the Bears welcomed a tremendous crowd of 26,000 fans to Wrigley Field for their championship matchup against the Giants. The game would end up being one of the greatest that Grandpa ever played or coached in. The Bears took an early lead on two field goals by "Automatic Jack" Manders. Then the Giants scored just before the half to take a 7–6 halftime advantage.

Early in the third quarter, Manders again kicked a chip-shot 28-yard field goal to give the Bears a 9–7 lead. But the Giants answered when Max Krause scored a touchdown to make it 14–9. As the third quarter drew to a close, the Bears marched downfield to the Giants' 8-yard line. Bronko Nagurski took a handoff and appeared as if he was going to plunge into the line. As he got to the line of scrimmage, however, he jumped up and lobbed a pass to Bill Karr, who took it into the end zone, giving the Bears a 16–14 advantage at the end of the third quarter.

The fourth quarter turned out to be a nail-biter for the Bears. Matching what the Bears did in the third quarter, the Giants drove to the Bears' 8-yard line. New York's All-Pro halfback, Ken Strong, attempted to sweep left, but found himself trapped, so he whirled around and tossed the ball back to the quarterback, Harry Newman. Bears defenders surrounded Newman, but somehow he got away, scrambled to the right sideline, and threw a desperation pass toward the goal line. Strong grabbed the pass at the 1-yard line and crossed the goal line as the Giants regained the lead 21–16—the fifth lead change of the game.

But the Bears had more razzle-dazzle up their sleeves. Nagurski again faked a plunge into the line before throwing over the middle, this time to Hewitt. Hewitt managed to run a few steps before the Giants secondary converged on him. So Hewitt lateraled the ball to Karr, who was trailing Hewitt on the play. Karr sprinted downfield along the right sideline and only had to beat Ken Strong. Out of the blue, Ronzani appeared and flattened Strong with a beautiful block, enabling Karr to tally the go-ahead touchdown.

Simply the Best

From 1938 to 1942, the NFL featured all-star games—a prelude to today's Pro Bowl contest—that pitted a collection of NFL all-stars against the team that had won the NFL championship. These games were held shortly after the NFL title game, either in late December or early January.

Just two weeks after the Japanese bombed Pearl Harbor to thrust the United States into World War II, the Bears defeated the New York Giants 37–9 to win the 1941 title—their second consecutive league crown. Grandpa decided to speak to the team before it played the NFL all-stars in early January 1942 at the Polo Grounds. When he addressed the team, he told team members that the 1941 Chicago Bears were, in his mind, the best team he had ever been involved with and the culmination of his dreams. It was an unforgettable experience for both him and the team, and he was overcome with emotion.

That score gave the Bears a 23–21 lead, but the Giants threw one last scare into the Bears on the final play of the game. Newman threw a 38-yard pass to running back Dale Burnett, who appeared to be in the clear. But Red Grange, who had developed into one of the game's greatest defensive players after achieving earlier fame as a runner, closed in on Burnett from his safety position. Burnett intended to have Grange tackle him; he would then lateral the ball to one of his teammates running alongside of him. Luckily for the Bears, Burnett was not in position to throw a block. Grange cleverly tackled Burnett high, trapping the ball against each player's chest. Burnett wasn't able to lateral the ball, both players fell to the ground, and the gun sounded. The Bears won the game and the NFL championship 23–21.

Members of each team received a bonus for playing in the title game. Each Bears player pocketed $210.34 and each Giants player $140.22 for their efforts in one of the greatest football games ever played. This exciting battle between the NFL's top two teams helped professional football make a strong comeback in Chicago and elsewhere in the heart of the Depression. The Bears averaged 20,000 per game at Wrigley Field, with box seats selling for $2.20 each and bleacher seats for $1. Overall, 280,000 spectators saw games between the Bears and their opponents that year.

The 1934 season turned out to be another memorable year in Chicago Bears history. It was the inaugural year for the College All-Star Game, which featured a squad of senior college all-stars going up against the team that had won the NFL championship the previous year. The game, sponsored by the *Chicago Tribune*, was developed by Arch Ward, the *Tribune* sports editor who helped launch the Major League Baseball All-Star Game in 1933.

However, it was Grandpa who initially approached Ward with the suggestion that a football all-star game would be a great idea. Many college coaches maintained that a good college team would destroy a good professional team. This argument irritated Grandpa, who was convinced that an NFL team, with its superior skill and additional years of experience, would be able to handle the best collegiate team ever assembled.

Ward wasn't receptive to Grandpa's idea at first, but his enthusiasm began to grow as Grandpa explained this game could become an outstanding annual attraction. Grandpa sealed the deal for Ward when he agreed to underwrite any losses that the *Tribune* might suffer. Well, the *Tribune*'s worries were needless. The game, which ended up a scoreless tie, was played at Soldier Field and drew a crowd of nearly 79,500.

The Bears breezed through the 1934 regular season, going 13–0 and winning the Western Division. Although they bowed to the Giants in

Easing the Pain

Bob Snyder played briefly for the Bears, backing up the great Sid Luckman at quarterback and also kicking three field goals in the 1941 NFL Championship Game. But at 4:00 AM on Sunday, November 5, 1939, he received the phone call that is every parent's nightmare. His wife Bobbie gave him the sad news that their eight-day-old son had suddenly died. Snyder wanted to rush home, but Bobbie advised him to play the game scheduled for that day and come home afterward.

Ray Nolting, Snyder's roommate, was the only player who knew of the couple's tragedy.

Later that afternoon, the Bears played the Green Bay Packers at Wrigley Field. Snyder kicked a field goal in the Bears' 30–27 victory over their rivals.

After the season, Snyder went to the Bears' office and met with Grandpa to sign a contract for 1940. Grandpa handed Snyder an envelope.

When Snyder left Grandpa's office, he looked in the envelope and saw a check for $1,000. Snyder was not due a bonus in his contract, so he went back into the office and asked Grandpa why he had given him a $1,000 check. Grandpa told Snyder to use it in order to take care of the funeral expenses for his son. They both started to cry a bit, and they hugged each other.

the title game 30–13, some believed at that time the '34 Bears were the greatest football team ever assembled. Grandpa just smiled, but he didn't refute that statement, even when asked about it later.

One big reason for all the accolades was a rookie halfback from Tennessee named Beattie Feathers. As soon as Grandpa and the Bears saw Feathers, they knew he was destined for stardom. Feathers, a tough 210-pounder, exhibited great agility and speed. However, he had never played in any offense other than the single wing at Tennessee, and he tended to dally a bit behind his blockers until daylight appeared—then he would take off. The Bears, of course, used the T formation with a man in motion, but Grandpa added a single-wing series to take full advantage of Feathers' skills.

Feathers, paired with Nagurski's blocking, made for a sensational duo. Feathers became the first player in NFL history to gain 1,000 yards during a regular season. It would take 13 years before another NFL running back eclipsed the 1,000-yard plateau.

Chapter 7

INSIDE THE BEARS' DEN

ver the years, I've collected countless stories about many of the greatest players and moments in Bears history, as well as the interactions people often had with my grandfather. Here are just a few.

CUTTING HIS TEETH

"Bullet Bill" Osmanski, a fullback who was the Bears' second first-round pick in 1939, attended dental school at Northwestern University while he played for the team. Ironically, Osmanski—a member of the NFL's All-Decade Team in the 1940s who rambled for a 68-yard touchdown run during the Bears' historic 73–0 NFL championship victory in 1940 over Washington—got his teeth knocked out. He later became a licensed dentist.

NOSE PROBLEM? NO PROBLEM!

Halfback George McAfee, who was a member of the NFL's All-Decade Team in the 1940s, once wrote this about Grandpa: "One thing I remember about Mr. Halas: I took myself out of a game; Mr. Halas asked why. I told him I think I broke my nose. Mr. Halas asked, 'Are you sure?' I said, 'Well…maybe.' He told me to go back in until I'm sure."

BOONE TIMES

In 1948, running back J.R. Boone arrived in Chicago for his first training camp. But Boone, a Tulsa product, didn't know about daylight saving time because they didn't use it in Oklahoma, so he didn't bother to change his watch. That resulted in his missing the bus to camp.

There he stood, outside of Wrigley Field, an hour late. He called the team office and was told that he would have to take the milk run train to Rensselaer, Indiana. Boone was a little embarrassed and plenty scared.

But everything worked out for the best. Some of the coaches met him at the train and gave him a warm welcome. However, a few of Boone's new teammates, as well as the press, thought he was one of the coaches' sons because it looked like he was too small to be a player.

That perception didn't faze Boone, who fondly recalled the inspiration he received from Grandpa on the sideline. Grandpa had Boone stand by him during games in which Boone didn't play, and talked to him about what was happening on the field and why. Grandpa, who encouraged Boone on many occasions to be a coach, ended up being a role model for Boone in his coaching, business, and personal life.

AN AGENT OF CHANGE

Jim Canady, who played for the Bears in 1948 and 1949, described how Grandpa always worked to change a situation if a particular set of circumstances didn't sit well with him.

Canady once wrote, "One day near the beginning of fall training camp in 1948, Mr. Halas announced that Paddy Driscoll would be looking after things for a brief period because Mr. Halas had to see about resolving a personal problem. He climbed into his Buick and left camp. Several days later he returned and took up directing our practice. Later that same day, in a player meeting, he saw fit to explain his sudden departure and absence. Rents were frozen during the National Emergency of the 1940s (there was a nationwide housing crisis after World War II) and landlords were held to then current charges.

"The war had ended and it loosed profiteering in the real estate market. Mr. Halas told us that his landlord had raised his and his neighbors' rent three times in the last year. It triggered a reaction. Mr. Halas, as a resident of the Edgewater Beach Apartments, went to his neighbors, put together a consortium, and bought the apartments. 'They will not raise my neighbors' or my own rent again. I have seen to that,' he declared. He had consummated a way to protect his neighbors and himself: he had acted. Typical."

Never Say Never

On September 24, 1950, the Bears played the 49ers in San Francisco and won the game 32–20. It was the 49ers' first NFL season. Originally a member of the All-American Football Conference, the 49ers were allowed to join the league after the AAFC merged with the NFL.

The Bears' trip back to Chicago was a little rough. Their flight ran into a thunderstorm that violently shook the plane. Grandpa sat next to Paddy Driscoll during the flight. Bears halfback Harper Davis heard Grandpa vow that the Bears would never fly again.

The Bears ended up facing the Los Angeles Rams in the playoffs that season. The game would be played in Los Angeles, and Grandpa, true to his word, had the team take a train out to the West Coast.

The Bears lost the game. And team flights promptly resumed after that defeat.

Do Not Disturb

The Bears played the Detroit Lions at Briggs Stadium (later known as Tiger Stadium) on October 28, 1951, and won the game 28–23. The next week, Bears rookie halfback Brad Rowland—a native of Texas who was inducted into the College Football Hall of Fame in 2008—ended up being late for practice. The team was standing at attention on the practice field with its back to Rowland listening to Grandpa expound at length on many important points. So Rowland tried to sneak onto the practice field without being spotted by either Grandpa or any of his teammates.

However, Rowland had to walk quite a distance to reach the area where Grandpa and the team had assembled. He had not gone 25 yards when a fellow Texan, defensive end Ed Sprinkle, spotted Rowland. Sprinkle began to clap his hands in cadence with each step Rowland took. If Rowland slowed his pace, Sprinkle slowed his applause. Soon, other Bears started clapping. It quickly reached a full team crescendo that provided Rowland with an unwanted standing ovation.

Interruptions like that tended to bother Grandpa, but this time he seemed particularly agitated because the Bears were in the hunt for a divisional championship. Plus, he would not tolerate any rookie showing up late for practice or a meeting, so he ran toward Rowland.

"Sorry, I'm late," Rowland mumbled to Grandpa.

The team erupted into thunderous applause. Rowland picked up a $35 fine.

SCHOOL BEFORE FOOTBALL

On January 17, 1952, the Bears selected end Bill McColl in the third round of the NFL Draft. McColl, who played collegiately at Stanford, met with Grandpa at the Arizona Biltmore Resort & Spa to negotiate his rookie contract. McColl signed a unique contract with the Bears that enabled him to attend medical school at the University of Chicago and make his medical training a priority over football.

McColl played for the Bears from 1952 to 1959. He became an orthopedic surgeon and went on to be a missionary doctor. His son Milt followed in his footsteps. Milt played linebacker for the San Francisco 49ers and Los Angeles Raiders and appeared in two Super Bowls during the 1980s before also becoming a doctor.

PROTOCOL TAKES A BACK SEAT TO KINDNESS

It was quite hot when the Bears' summer training camp got under way at St. Joseph's College in Rensselaer, Indiana, in 1952. The Bears dressed in shorts for the morning practice and donned full gear for the afternoon session.

Grandpa allowed fans to watch practice and allowed players to visit with them and sign autographs before practice started. Players, however, were not allowed to talk to fans once practice began.

One afternoon at practice, fullback John "Kayo" Dottley caught a pass along the sideline. As he was running back to the huddle, he heard a small voice yelling, "Mr. Dottley, Mr. Dottley!"

Kayo looked around and spotted a little boy in a wheelchair. Kayo knew the rule, but he just had to stop and ask what he could do for the boy. His father said Kayo was the boy's favorite player and that the little boy wanted Kayo to sign his junior football. Kayo asked if the boy could wait until after practice to sign the football, but his dad said the boy was very ill and the heat was bad for him.

As Kayo was signing the ball, Grandpa tapped him on the shoulder and said, "John Dottley, what are you doing? You know the rule. Now get your butt back on the field."

Then Grandpa noticed the little boy. He looked down and asked, "What is your name, son?" The little boy said, "Billy."

"Billy, how would you like to have a real Chicago Bears ball signed by John Dottley and me?" Grandpa asked him.

Billy replied, "Coach, that would make me the happiest boy in the world."

"Well, Dottley, go get him a ball and let's sign it for Billy," Grandpa shouted. Grandpa picked Billy up and gave him a big hug and the ball.

From that day on, Dottley—the first player in University of Mississippi history to rush for more than 1,000 yards in two seasons—respected and loved Grandpa. And Grandpa felt the same about Kayo.

A "WASH" OUT

Washington "Wash" Serini, a guard who played for the Bears starting in 1948, didn't make the team in 1952, and the Green Bay Packers ended up signing him. That September, the Bears traveled to play Green Bay—with Serini in a Packers uniform—and won 24–14.

Then in November, the Bears hosted the Packers at Wrigley Field. This time around, the Bears lost 41–28, and Serini played a major role in helping Green Bay notch the win. Serini ripped the Bears and Grandpa in the locker room after the game.

During a team meeting the following Tuesday, Grandpa posted game articles from the newspapers on the blackboard and said, "Men, 'Wash' had his day, but this was not a good thing to do."

PREDICTING GREATNESS

In December 1953, Tom Roggeman—an offensive guard who was captain of the 1952 Big Ten Conference cochampion Purdue Boilermakers—paid Grandpa a visit to negotiate a contract. He had recently joined the U.S. Marine Corps and sat in front of the big desk in Grandpa's office wearing his military greens. While Tom sat in the office, he looked at pictures on the wall of championship teams and NFL greats.

Roggeman sprang to his feet as Grandpa entered his office. Grandpa did all the talking. He talked mainly about his beloved Bears, then he zeroed in on all the offensive linemen he already had on the roster, including rookie offensive tackle Stan Jones.

After Roggeman listened to Grandpa talk about Jones' outstanding abilities, Grandpa got around to how he thought Roggeman would fit into the Bears' roster. Roggeman signed a contract that day, but shortly thereafter, he was shipped to Korea, where he served at times on the demilitarized zone that separates North and South Korea (the Korean War ended in July 1953).

Following his discharge from the Marines, Roggeman reported to the Bears. At training camp in Rensselaer, he finally got to meet Stan

Jones, the man Grandpa raved about. Jones and Roggeman became lifetime friends. Jones, by the way, lived up to Grandpa's predictions of greatness. He was a perennial All-Pro and was inducted into the Pro Football Hall of Fame in 1991.

BED AND BENITO MUSSOLINI

Don Kindt, a defensive back who played for the Bears from 1947 to 1955, served in the army during World War II and was stationed in Italy. The night before VE Day (May 8, 1945), Kindt slept in the bed of Italian dictator Benito Mussolini, who was killed days earlier trying to escape to Switzerland.

Another interesting story involving Kindt was mentioned in an October 2002 piece by Bob Wolfley, a columnist for the *Milwaukee Journal Sentinel*. Kindt, who starred at the University of Wisconsin, happened to be late for his very first game with the Bears up in Green Bay.

A Bears team doctor, who was going to give Kindt a shot of Novocain to relieve pain in his bad ankle, arrived late at East Stadium. After getting the shot, Kindt ran from a nearby high school locker room where the Bears dressed to the stadium, but the ticket takers wouldn't let him in.

"Later I heard Curly Lambeau, the Green Bay coach, had given instructions not to let any opposing players in if they were late," Kindt told Wolfley.

Grandpa chewed out Kindt, who had missed the first seven minutes of the game. Grandpa did later insert him into the game, though.

JOHNNY MORRIS WEIGHS IN

Johnny Morris, one of the most prolific receivers in Bears history, joined the squad in 1958 out of the University of California–Santa Barbara. Morris, who became a Chicago television sportscaster after he retired from the game, made clutch catches and ended up becoming the team's all-time leading receiver with 5,059 career yards (Morris accumulated 1,200 yards in 1964 alone).

Morris wasn't big. So one day before team weigh-ins, Morris put five-pound weights under his arms so he would appear to be 10 pounds heavier!

Hot and Cold

In early November 1958, the Bears played the Los Angeles Rams at the Coliseum. Autumn in Los Angeles was nothing like autumn in Chicago; the temperature on the field was 116 degrees. During warm-ups, Bears rookie assistant coach Chuck Mather wore a short-sleeved shirt. Grandpa ran over to Mather and said, "Kid, put your jacket on. The players will think it's hot."

A few weeks later, the Bears played the Pittsburgh Steelers in Pittsburgh. It was extremely cold. This time, Mather wore a long, heavy coat with a fur collar. Just before the team was about to take the field for warm-ups, Grandpa took one look at Mather and said, "Hey, kid. Take that coat off and put on a jacket. The players will think it's cold."

Alex Karras' Brother Makes the Right Choice

Just before the 1960 season, offensive guard Ted Karras, who had played for the Pittsburgh Steelers in 1958 and 1959, got a call from a secretary in the Bears' front office to set up a meeting with Grandpa. Grandpa wanted to sign Karras; he had $7,000 and a $500 bonus waiting for him.

But Karras hesitated. He told Grandpa the Cardinals had offered him $8,000.

Grandpa asked, "Who would you rather play for? The Cardinals at $8,000 or the Bears at $7,500?"

The Cardinals had just suffered through a 2–10 season in 1959 and could not compete with the Bears in Chicago, so their owner, Violet Bidwill, decided to move the team to St. Louis in 1960.

Karras decided an extra $500 wasn't worth moving and playing for a team that was struggling. He signed with the Bears and ended up being the starting left guard on the Bears' 1963 championship team.

Interestingly, Karras is the brother of Alex Karras, who enjoyed a 12-year NFL career with the Detroit Lions. Alex later became an actor, with roles in the movies *Blazing Saddles, Porky's,* and *Against All Odds.* He also was a color commentator on ABC's *Monday Night Football.*

The NFL Expands Its Horizons

Grandpa oversaw the NFL expansion committee in 1959, and persuaded Clint Murchison and his partners to buy a franchise in Dallas. Grandpa put them in touch with Tex Schramm, who became the team's general manager. Tex then hired Tom Landry to be Dallas' head coach.

In addition to the regular draft of college players, the league instituted an expansion draft to provide the Cowboys with veteran players to help bolster their roster. The Bears took Southern Methodist quarterback Don Meredith in the third round of the 1960 NFL Draft, but traded him to Schramm and Dallas for future draft picks. Meredith was a star for the Cowboys for nine seasons. He was named Player of the Year in 1966 and went to the Pro Bowl three times.

The NFL expanded from 12 to 13 teams with the addition of the Cowboys in 1960. The league also faced direct competition from a rival league for the first time in decades as the new American Football League made its debut. The AFL at that time consisted of the Boston Patriots, Buffalo Bills, Dallas Texans, Denver Broncos, Houston Oilers, Los Angeles Chargers, New York Titans, and Oakland Raiders.

Fire Guts Bears' Office

The Bears' offices at 233 West Madison Street in Chicago caught fire and burned in late January 1961. Sadly, Grandpa stored a lot of memorabilia and items from Bears history there that were lost when the fire swept through that building. The fire broke out at about 5:00 PM and Bears assistant coach Chuck Mather saw the fire on television in Wilmette and went to the site. He and Grandpa stood across the street from the fire.

Mather asked, "Coach, isn't this awful?" After a few moments, Grandpa replied, "Let's go away." He never mentioned the fire again. The next day, the Bears moved a few doors down to 173 West Madison Street.

Da Coach Has a Great Game

En route to their 1963 NFL championship, the Bears visited the Pittsburgh Steelers in late November. Tight end—and future Bears head coach and Hall of Famer—Mike Ditka caught a pass in the fourth quarter, broke six tackles, and set up a field goal that would tie the game. Roger Leclerc kicked the ball between the uprights from 18 yards out, and the Bears salvaged a 17–17 tie with the Steelers. Ditka—sixth in the NFL in pass receptions during 1963 with 59—finished with seven receptions for 146 yards.

Weight and See

My father recalled this story about Stan Jones:

"After the Bears had won the 1963 championship, Mayor [Richard J.] Daley invited the team to city hall to show appreciation. He said that a gift to everyone would be forthcoming.

"Stan and [his wife] Darlis went home and waited for it. With the playoff money, they bought a glass table. Every day he would ask Darlis, 'Did the gift come from the mayor?' The answer was 'no' for several weeks.

"One day Darlis said, 'Stan, Mayor Daley's gift arrived.' In his haste to open the package, it slipped out of his hands and broke the glass table. The gift was a City of Chicago paperweight."

UNDERAGE SIGNING

Before training camp in 1964, former NFL running back Whizzer White told Grandpa about Andy Livingston, who attended the same high school as White had in Mesa, Arizona. Livingston had not been playing in college due to some problems off the field, but he was a very talented running back. Following much discussion, Grandpa let him come to camp. After a few days in camp, Grandpa sent White a contract to have Livingtson's mother sign since Livingston was still under age. Livingston played for the Bears from 1964 through 1968, then played briefly for the New Orleans Saints.

MAY I HAVE THE ENVELOPE, PLEASE...

The Bears gathered in the lobby of Chicago's Edgewater Beach Hotel one Friday afternoon in late August 1964, hours before they were to play the St. Louis Cardinals in the Armed Forces Benefit Game at Soldier Field. Linebacker Jim Purnell was sitting on a couch, and Grandpa sat next to him.

Grandpa said, "Jim, I have some good news for you. We want you to sign a contract to be a player on the 1964 team."

Purnell said, "Coach, that's great news, and I can't think of anything that would make me happier."

With that, Grandpa reached inside his suit jacket and pulled out some papers, which he quickly looked through. He said, "Jim, I thought I had a blank player contract with me, but it looks as though I don't."

At this point, Grandpa pulled out a blank envelope that had Gus Kasapis' name on it, which had been scratched out. (Kasapis, a defensive tackle, had been cut earlier that day.)

Grandpa said, "I guess this will have to do" and he began to write: "It is agreed that the Chicago Bears will employ Jim..."

At this point Grandpa looked at Purnell with great intensity. Purnell quickly realized that Grandpa couldn't remember his last name. Without missing a beat, Grandpa continued writing—leaving blank the space where Jim's last name should have appeared—"...for the 1964 season for the sum of $8,500." Grandpa signed his name and then handed the envelope to Jim. It was the only document ever produced that proved Purnell was officially a member of the 1964 Chicago Bears.

BLIND DECISION

When my eye doctor, Jonathan Rubenstein, was a boy, he went to Bears games with his father. Rubenstein's sister complained that she never got to go to a game. The weather happened to be cold and rainy on December 12, 1965, so Rubenstein said that his sister could go to the game against the San Francisco 49ers in his place.

Well, Jonathan undoubtedly wished he could have attended the game his sister witnessed. The Bears throttled the 49ers 61–20 as Gale Sayers scored six touchdowns.

SOMETHING SPECIAL

Linebacker Bill George called Dad one morning in February 1966 and asked him to come down to a golf driving range near Rosemont, Illinois. George owned the range with his partners, Mike Ditka and Joe Marconi, who played fullback for the Bears until 1966.

When Dad got there, George said, "I want to show you something."

George took Dad over to a dog run where there was an Irish setter. Bill said, "This dog was given to one of our taxi squad people, Brian Piccolo, by a waitress. The dog was near death when Brian got him. We've been nursing him back. When he gets healthy and happy, I'm gonna send him to my mother in Pennsylvania."

George then said to Dad, "The reason I've asked you to come down is because I want you to know that next season, I will not be with the Bears."

"What are you talking about, Bill?" Dad said. "I've heard the old man tell you that you are with him for life."

George said, "No. He's chosen a new middle linebacker, Dick Butkus. I've been here a long time and I'm leaving. What I want you to do is take care of this boy on the taxi squad, Brian Piccolo, because he's something special."

Dad said, "Bill, how can I take care of him? I don't work for the Bears."

"You'll find a way, and I'm giving him to you." George replied. "Take care of him."

George's words proved to be prophetic. Brian Piccolo went on to become a starting fullback for the Bears a few years later, and was paired in the same backfield with the great Gale Sayers. However, Sayers and

Brian Piccolo was one of the most courageous men to ever wear a Bears uniform.

the entire Bears family took Piccolo under their wings when he was diagnosed with cancer in 1969.

Piccolo sadly lost his battle with cancer in 1970. The following year, a movie about Piccolo's life, his friendship with Sayers, and his fight against cancer was released. *Brian's Song* received great reviews and national acclaim.

BILL WADE

Bill Wade, who quarterbacked the Bears to their 1963 NFL championship, was a great natural athlete. Wade played on the football, basketball, and baseball teams while attending Montgomery Bell Academy in Nashville. He was a single-wing tailback in football and a decent basketball player. He also played catcher, pitcher, shortstop, and center field for the baseball team.

Wade started at short during one particular game, but his team's starting pitcher that day walked the first six batters he faced in the first inning, and the team trailed 3–0. The coach summoned Wade to the mound. Wade's sinker was devastating that day, and he ended up striking out 21 batters. But his team was still losing 3–0 heading into the last inning, so Wade took matters into his own hands. He came to bat with the bases loaded and hit a grand slam to give his team a 4–3 victory. His teammates carried him off the field on their shoulders.

After graduating from high school, Wade stayed in Nashville and went to Vanderbilt University, where he quarterbacked the Commodores. He passed for 3,396 yards in his career—which stood as a school record for more than 30 years. He also earned second-team All-America honors and was named SEC Player of the Year in 1951.

Wade once threw a football 82 yards during a game against Arkansas. On that play, Wade scrambled behind the line of scrimmage; one of his receivers ran to the end zone, but came back because he thought Wade couldn't throw the ball that far. But Wade did, and when the ball landed in the end zone right where the receiver had been standing, it ended up being an incomplete pass instead of a touchdown.

Wade did make the baseball team at Vanderbilt, but he didn't get to play much because he was involved in spring football practice. The Los Angeles Rams made him the first overall pick of the 1952 NFL Draft. After serving two years in the navy, he received an offer to play baseball with the San Diego Padres of the Pacific Coast League during the Rams' off-season. However, the Rams wouldn't let him play pro baseball.

Wade played for the Rams from 1954 through 1960; he was then traded to the Bears. After the Bears won five straight to begin the 1963 season, they ended up suffering their first loss at San Francisco. During the flight home, Wade moved to the forward part of the plane and poured

Bill Wade led the Bears to the 1963 NFL title, and also taught me a thing or two about playing quarterback.

out his sorrows to Grandpa. Grandpa listened patiently and then asked, "Who do we play next week?"

Later, Wade wrote that Grandpa had a "great ability to constantly push forward and look ahead through hardship and defeat, heartache and disappointment."

The Bears won their next four games, tied two, and won two more. Then they beat the New York Giants in the NFL Championship Game 14–10 as Wade scored both touchdowns on quarterback sneaks.

Wade became a player/coach in 1967. During training camp one day, some of the ball boys got involved in a tremendous water fight in a bathroom at one of the team's dormitories. Shower stalls were plugged, and water overflowed. Wade walked into the melee, surveyed the situation, and calmly said, "If you put the washroom back into its original condition, I won't tell Coach Halas."

Everyone accepted his offer.

The calendar turned to 1968, and Grandpa asked Wade to call him on May 1 and tell him if he wanted to continue with the team. That day, Wade told Grandpa that he wanted to retire in order to spend more time at home because of family issues. Grandpa tried to talk him out of it, and said, "If you agree to come back, I think something wonderful will happen."

Wade said no thank you. Unbeknownst to him, Grandpa might have eventually handed him the job of head coach.

After Wade hung up the phone, he cried for three hours. For the first time in 33 years, Wade was out of football.

On May 27, 1968, Grandpa announced his retirement from coaching.

Several years later, Wade's first wife attended her high school reunion. She ended up divorcing Bill and marrying her high school sweetheart. Bill got remarried in 1991 to Mary Ellen Clinton; the ceremony took place at the First Presbyterian Church in Nashville,

Tennessee. The guests at Bill's second wedding agreed it was wonderful to see him happy.

HAPPY ANNIVERSARY

Mom and Dad celebrated their 25th wedding anniversary on February 2, 1968. Mugs threw a wonderful surprise party for them. During the party, Grandpa took the microphone and spoke directly to Dad's mother, who was in the dining room. He said, "Kit, I would like you to know that I'm as proud of Ed as I am of my boy Mugs."

My mom, Grandpa Halas, my dad, my uncle Mugs, and Grandma Min

THE BEARS' "DISASTER PLAN"

Grandpa and Dad's first attempt to work together didn't go very well. My dad had worked at May & Halas, my grandfather's sporting goods store, in 1949 but didn't enjoy it very much. But several years later, Grandpa started talking to Dad about joining the Bears. (Grandpa waited until Mom and Dad had been married 24 years and produced 11 children, figuring their marriage was fairly secure by that time!)

Dad said, "Well, Coach, how will Mugs [George Halas Jr.] feel about this? He's your heir; he's going to run the Bears."

Grandpa said, "This is Mugs' idea."

So Dad agreed to join the Bears, and he went to work for the team in the summer of 1967, serving as a liaison among management, coaches, and players.

During Dad's first day with the Bears, Brian Piccolo came up to him and said, "Don't worry, Big Ed; I'll square you away with the players."

Piccolo did just that.

Later that first day, Mugs called Dad into his office and asked, "What do you know about the National Football League?"

"I know they play football, Mugs," Dad replied.

Mugs asked, "What do you know about the 'disaster plan'?"

Dad said, "I never heard of it."

"We have a disaster plan in the league," Mugs said. "I never want you to fly on the team plane. I want you to fly commercial. Dad and I will go on the team plane. If the plane goes down, the disaster plan goes into effect.

"You're allowed to take any assistant coach as your head coach. Take Phil Bengston of Green Bay. You're allowed to take any backup quarterback as your quarterback. Take Zeke Bratkowski of Green Bay.

"Each of the other teams will have to give you three players. Just take anyone they give you. That isn't important.

"Here's the important thing: the week the plane goes down [the team] won't be able to play. Make certain that you make up that game at the end of the season."

"Okay, Mugs," Dad said. "Suppose my plane goes down?"

"Then we don't have a problem," Mugs replied.

DEATHS IN THE FAMILY

Brian Piccolo fell gravely ill in 1969 and had to fly to New York City for treatment. His wife Joy needed to be with him, so Dad asked me to fly with their daughters, Lori, Traci, and Kristi—ages three, two, and one, respectively, at that time—to Atlanta to stay with Joy's parents.

On Tuesday, June 16, 1970, Piccolo died. He was just 26 years old. He wore No. 41 when he played for the Bears, and there are a couple of interesting parallels associated with that number. When Charlton Heston was on the slave ship in the movie *Ben Hur*, he was No. 41. When Roger Bannister became the first man to ever run a mile under four minutes, he also wore No. 41.

But Brian Piccolo was our favorite No. 41. He is one of 13 Bears to have his number retired. The others are Bronko Nagurski (3), George McAfee (5), Grandpa (7), Willie Galimore (28), Walter Payton (34), Gale Sayers (40), Sid Luckman (42), Dick Butkus (51), Bill Hewitt (56), Bill George (61), Clyde Turner (66), and Red Grange (77).

On October 13 of that year, Mike Rabold, an offensive guard, also died. He was only 33 years old. Rabold broke into the NFL in 1959 with the Detroit Lions, then played for St. Louis and Minnesota before finishing his career in a Bears uniform.

Rabold had also attended Indiana University and helped me get into McNutt Quad at IU.

SEEING DOUBLE

The Bears traveled to South Bend, Indiana, for a preseason game against the Cleveland Browns in 1971. The late Jack Warden was on the sideline that day filming scenes for the movie *Brian's Song* wearing a wide-brim hat. (Jack would go on to win an Emmy Award for his portrayal of Grandpa).

Chicago Sun-Times columnist Jack Griffin—one of my favorite sportswriters and a good friend of the family—happened to be in the press box. Reporters covering the game who didn't know Warden was playing Grandpa in the movie asked Griffin if Grandpa was coming back to coach.

Griffin didn't tell the reporters that it was Jack Warden on the sideline, not George Halas. He just said, "Yes."

STRAIGHT FROM THE HIP

One day Russ Thompson, an offensive tackle who played for the Bears from 1936 to 1939, read about a trip Grandpa made to England for an artificial hip replacement in 1971. Realizing that a hip replacement could be an option for him, Thompson called Grandpa to find out how and whom he should contact in England.

Thompson talked to Grandpa and found out Grandpa had brought two doctors from England back with him; those doctors were now practicing at Illinois Masonic Hospital in Chicago. After hearing that, Thompson and his wife Mary Jo decided to come to Chicago and make arrangements for the surgery.

While Thompson was recovering in the hospital, Grandpa called and brought flowers. Later, as Thompson was learning to walk on crutches, Grandpa visited him and brought Thompson his old crutches, which pleased him very much. That's when Mary Jo discovered there was a compassionate side to the famous coach.

"Our family and the eastern half of Wyoming have always been adamant fans of the Bears and George Halas," Mary Jo wrote in 2002. "His leadership of the hip replacement from England for all of the United States was another of his outstanding contributions. It too should be celebrated."

Mac Attack

On August 20, 1972, the Bears played the New England Patriots in a preseason game and attempted a fake field goal at one point during the contest. Bobby Douglass, the Bears' rugged, athletic, left-handed quarterback who also was the holder on field goals, rolled to his right while Mac Percival, the kicker, drifted out to the left. Douglass threw the ball and Percival caught it. But as Percival hauled in the pass, he had a flashback to a year or two earlier when the Bears ran the same play. Head coach Abe Gibron reprimanded Percival for running out of bounds, so this time, Percival cut back toward the middle of the field.

Percival picked up about 20 yards before a Patriots linebacker hit him high while another hit him low. Mac was dazed, but Dick Butkus came to his defense. Butkus leaped over Percival and slugged one of the linebackers. A huge brawl broke out on top of Mac. Percival crawled out from under the melee and made it to the sideline where teammate and punter Bobby Joe Green laughed uproariously at him.

Going with the Flow

Jack Pardee became the Bears' new head coach prior to the 1975 season, replacing Abe Gibron. I sat at the kitchen table with Mom eating breakfast on the day the Bears and Gibron parted ways. She started crying and said, "I don't care who the next coach is. I'm not going to get to know him very well because I don't want to have to go through this again."

But she did. She got to know Pardee, Neill Armstrong, Mike Ditka, Dave Wannstedt, and Dick Jauron, and she supported them all. Now she supports Lovie Smith.

Saying Good-Bye to Rita

In early September of 1975, Rita Hauk—a woman who became good friends with Grandpa—died. In the September 17, 1975, edition of the

Chicago Sun-Times, sportswriter Jack Griffin wrote about their friendship without mentioning either one's name:

"Sometimes, you see something beautiful, and you feel warmer for the sight of it. But then there is a sadness when it must end.

"I won't tell you the guy's name. He wouldn't like it. But then I suspect you'll have guessed who he is by the time I have finished.

"A number of years ago, his wife died. They had been married a long time and they loved each other very much. That must have been the first hurt, a hot knife drawn across his chest. But I didn't know him then.

"He lived alone. His children and his grandchildren would visit. But it wasn't the same thing. Then a few years ago, he met this lady and, you'd better believe, baby, I mean a lady.

"I don't think they were drawn together by loneliness. There was just something between them. It's possible for a man to have known two

My grandfather and Rita Hauk

women, and not have the love of one diminish another. He was nearly 80 then, she in her sixties. They were beautiful to watch together.

"A week or so ago, she died suddenly. It was all so quick. Just snap your fingers, and she was gone. And my friend had another pain to bear.

"Maybe you've guessed by now who he is. I don't care if you haven't. I didn't write this column for you. I wrote it for my friend. I want him to know how sorry I am."

CORNERBACK'S CORNER

Virgil Livers played cornerback for the Bears from 1975 to 1979. The one thing Livers remembers most about Grandpa was his continued involvement with the daily operations of the team—especially knowing tidbits about his players.

During a birthday party for Grandpa, Livers went up to him, seeking his autograph on a photo of him in his baseball uniform. Grandpa looked up and asked his name. Virgil responded, "Virgil Livers."

Grandpa immediately said, "Oh, yes. You're that young fellow from Western Kentucky with all of that speed."

Virgil said, "Yes, I am from Western."

Livers was amazed that Grandpa knew something about him. Strange as it seems, that has always meant a lot to Livers.

BOB HOPE

On February 10, 1976, the Chicago Boys Clubs presented the Chicagoan of the Year Award to Grandpa at the Conrad Hilton Hotel. Friends were asked to write letters of congratulation. Here is what Bob Hope wrote:

"I regret very much that I can't be there to honor a fellow actor. I have watched you for many years destroying hats on the sidelines. I don't know how much stock you have in Stetson, but they should give you a chapeau for the rest of your life.

"Why you didn't get an Emmy for your histrionics at the 50-yard line, the 40-yard line, the 30-yard line, the 20-yard line, and the other side of the field—I will never understand.

"You are a legend. A man that deserves any tribute brought your way because you started this wonderful game of football. In fact, I understand you are the guy who caught the original pig and laced him up.

"I will never forget our experiences together in the South Pacific when you were the Special Services Officer for the navy. You proved then how big your heart is and it is the thing that I hope will keep you going for many, many years because you are a great asset to our way of life.

Bob Hope honored my grandfather at a banquet in 1976.

"Enjoy yourself tonight and don't think of last season. If you do think of it, think of me; I bought a condominium in downtown Beirut. I just wish I was there to help applaud and cheer you."

PLAYOFF-BOUND

The Bears went into their 1977 regular-season finale at Giants Stadium against the New York Giants with an opportunity to go to the playoffs for the first time since their 1963 NFL championship season. They had won five straight going into this game, and the great Walter Payton was nothing short of spectacular during this winning streak. Payton, who led the NFL in rushing that season with 1,852 yards, averaged just over 173 yards per game over that five-game span—including racking up 275 yards against Minnesota on November 20, which stood as an NFL single-game record for many years.

Bob Thomas' 32-yard field goal in the first quarter and Robin Earl's four-yard touchdown run in the fourth quarter set up a 9–9 tie with the Giants at the end of regulation.

Thomas describes the situation from that point:

"We were in sudden-death overtime, the score knotted at nine apiece, and we needed to win to get into the playoffs as a wild-card entry, and the Bears had not been to the playoffs for 14 years. There was only one overtime period because this was a regular-season game, and a tie would do us no good. The pressure was mounting.

"As [quarterback] Bob Avellini and Walter Payton engineered one final drive, my teammates on the sideline were offering all kinds of words of encouragement [to me]. Bob Parsons, our punter, obviously not a psychology major at Penn State, told me if I didn't make the kick he would personally break my neck.

"We got close and time was running out and we did not have any timeouts left. I remember Walter Payton and Roland Harper [Payton's backfield mate] appeared to be making angels in the snow out there to clear a spot for me to kick. And to me it seemed like I never stopped

Sweetness

Several hours after the Chicago Bears drafted Walter Payton in the first round of the 1975 NFL Draft, I drove to O'Hare Airport to meet him. However, he ended up not making the flight.

Walter Payton was the best football player I have ever seen. He ran, he blocked, he caught, he passed...and he tackled if he threw an interception on those occasions when he was called to throw a halfback-option pass.

Payton played halfback, fullback, quarterback, wide receiver, kickoff returner, cheerleader, receptionist, and coach. There was a lot of Harpo Marx in Walter Payton. When reporters interviewed him, he often picked their pockets. He was the best on the team at throwing rolled-up socks in the locker room after practice. And he did a great impersonation of Buckwheat.

One of the things that kept me busy was speaking at Walter Payton award ceremonies (too many to count). It was a privilege to have him in a Chicago Bears uniform. He personified the word *superstar*, and was one of the most humble and soft-spoken gentlemen you'd ever meet. The day after he rushed for 275 yards in a game, for example, he volunteered for the scout team.

moving from the time our head coach, Jack Pardee, pushed me onto the field until my foot propelled the winning field goal [28 yards] through the uprights with just a few seconds left to play.

"Avellini, my holder, raised his fist in jubilation. Parsons and center Dan Neal were rolling on the tundra like polar bear cubs. I was hoisted onto my teammates' shoulders in a state which could only be described as euphoria."

Thomas' kick gave the Bears a 12–9 victory, and the Bears advanced to the playoffs as a wild-card entry by virtue of a tiebreaker over the Washington Redskins. Ironically, Pardee left the Bears a week after they lost to Dallas in a divisional playoff game to become the Redskins' head coach.

DIVINE INTERVENTION

I attended a Bears Bible study on a night in early April 1979, when the wind was so strong that windows were blown out of the John Hancock Center. During the drive home, my car died. Fortunately, some kind youngsters in a pickup truck gave me a ride back to Doug and Nancy Plank's home. The Planks loaned me one of their cars and then met the tow truck at my car.

"WE ONLY HELP OURSELVES BY HELPING OTHERS"

On a June day in 1981, Grandpa wrote to Don Mullins, who had played defensive back for the Bears in 1961 and 1962:

Dear Don:

Paul Orseck sent me the article from the May 17th edition of *The Houston Post* telling of your involvement with the Ronald McDonald House in Houston.

As I read the article my heart swelled with pride because of you. As I read the article my heart swelled equally for you because of the loss of your son. I know what the loss of a son means.

I promise you all the time and energy you gave so freely to bring Houston's Ronald McDonald House to reality will be repaid to you a thousand times over by the good Lord. We only help ourselves by helping others, and by helping others our lives have dignity and meaning. God bless you and warmest personal regards.

Sincerely,

George S. Halas

ASK AND YOU SHALL RECEIVE $5

The George Halas Junior Center was dedicated at Loyola University in Chicago on September 2, 1982. Bears guard Dr. Joe Kopcha happened to be standing near me during the dedication, and he complained to me about how difficult it was to get even a $5 raise from Grandpa. So I promptly gave Dr. Kopcha $5.

DITKA'S COACHING DEBUT

Mike Ditka's first regular-season game as head coach of the Bears took place on September 12, 1982, against the Detroit Lions at the Pontiac Silverdome. Right before the opening kickoff, he said to the team, "All you have to do is want it as much as we know you want it. Do you want it that much?" Well, Ditka's passionate attempt to fire up the troops didn't resonate this particular day. The Bears lost 17–10.

Iron Mike's inaugural season certainly didn't go as well as he would have liked. The Bears finished 3–6 during a campaign that was shortened to nine games because of a 57-day players' strike. However, the Bears' fortunes would change dramatically after that.

Ditka led the Bears to six NFC Central titles over the next 10 years, and took them to the NFC Championship Game three times. Of course, he'll always be revered by Bears fans everywhere for guiding the team to Super Bowl XX and beating New England to win it all.

HURRY UP, OFFENSE!

On Sunday, December 18, 1983, the Bears hosted the Green Bay Packers at Soldier Field on a sunny but very cold afternoon. You could see steam rising off Lake Michigan. Defensive end Al Harris put Vaseline on his face and his arms—and it froze. Harris was also suffering from turf toe, but the cold turned out to be just what the doctor ordered; he couldn't feel it, and thus, he experienced no pain.

At one point during the game, Harris told the offense, "Hurry up and score or get off the field so the defense can play and stay warm."

The offense heeded Harris' instructions as the Bears won 23–21.

ACROSS THE POND

Fresh off their Super Bowl championship in January, the 1986 Bears traveled to London to face the Dallas Cowboys in an exhibition game at Wembley Stadium. I had a terrific week in London from July 31 through August 3. The Bears practiced at Crystal Palace, a residential area in south London where Steve Cram had set the world record in the 1,500-meter run in 1985.

Some of us also visited the Tower of London, where Sir Thomas More, the author of *Utopia*, had been imprisoned. Our guide explained that More's prison room was very spacious. The Bears, meanwhile, locked up Dallas 17–6.

A Classic Car

The original meeting that formed what is now the NFL took place on September 17, 1920, in Ralph Hay's Hupmobile Showroom in Canton, Ohio. In 1989, my brother Mike and I found a couple of Hupmobiles. One was showcased at the Bears' home game on September 17, 1989, in conjunction with the celebration of the team's 70th season. Before the game, my parents and Peg Holmes, Dutch Sternaman's daughter, rode onto the field in it.

Well-known gospel singer Amy Grant sang the national anthem that day. The Bears capped off the day by beating the Minnesota Vikings 38–7.

Happy Anniversary

On Saturday, March 3, 1990, Gretchen and I celebrated our sixth anniversary. The next day, we hopped in the car and headed out to Charlottesville, Virginia, to visit an old friend, Alan Swanson, his wife Donna, and their sons Danny and Allie.

Alan taught seventh-graders, so during our visit I sat in on his English class while he let me teach his history classes. We showed a video titled *George Halas and the Chicago Bears*. Then we talked about the history of the team and the National Football League.

Later, Alan told me that he hopes the McCaskeys never sell majority interest of the Bears. He said, "It's the only time you'll really do something together as a family."

Sign of the Times

The City of Chicago designated 20 locations with markers of distinction on September 23, 1997. One of the places marked was 4356 West Washington Boulevard, where Grandpa lived when he started the Bears. The marker read, "'Papa Bear' was synonymous with the Chicago Bears for a half-century as owner, coach, and general manager. He helped found the National Football League and turn pro football into mass entertainment."

Stolen Goods

My family and I were out on Thanksgiving Day in 1993 to watch the Bears defeat the Lions at the Pontiac Silverdome. While we were awat, thieves broke into our home and stole my Super Bowl ring. But thanks to some great police work, I got the ring back a few days later.

Remembering Sweetness

Walter Payton died on November 1, 1999, after battling liver disease and bile duct cancer. He was the best football player I have ever seen. He blocked; he tackled; he ran; he caught; he punted; he passed; and he kicked. Walter played halfback, but he was a fullback, quarterback, receiver, kick returner, cheerleader, receptionist, and coach, too.

He certainly was very elusive on and off the field—and well known for playing practical jokes. Payton would, for example, light firecrackers, take calls at the Bears' switchboard, untie referees' shoelaces, and disguise his voice to sound like a woman, then call his friends' wives and pretend to be "the other woman."

For example, when Walter answered the phone in my father's office, he'd say in a high, female-sounding voice, "This is Bernice. Mr. McCaskey can't come to the phone right now because I'm giving him a full body massage."

Walter Payton, signing a new contract with my brother Mike.

It was an honor and a privilege to have him in a Chicago Bears uniform. We can continue to extend his legacy through commitment to excellence and having a lot of fun.

PERSEVERANCE PAYS OFF

The Bears played their first game in a renovated Soldier Field on Monday, September 29, 2003. Unfortunately it wasn't a successful debut. The Green Bay Packers and Brett Favre handed the Bears a 38–23 defeat.

The Bears' quest to build a new stadium actually started in 1956—so it took a journey of nearly 50 years to reach that night. This odyssey reminded me of a quote from the late U.S. Admiral Hyman Rickover, the "Father of the Nuclear Navy," that appeared in a book by Warren Bennis and Burt Nanus, titled *Leaders*: "Nothing worthwhile can be accomplished without determination. In the early days of nuclear power, for example, getting approval to build the first nuclear submarine—the *Nautilus*—was almost as difficult as designing and building it. Good ideas are not adopted automatically. They must be driven into practice with courageous patience."

Hate It, Love It
The Bears traveled to New York to play the Giants at Giants Stadium on November 7, 2004. The Bears came out in an I formation in the fourth quarter, and general manager Jerry Angelo couldn't hide his disdain for what he was seeing on the field. "I hate that formation. I hate that formation," he huffed. But as Anthony Thomas ran 41 yards for a touchdown out of the I in the fourth quarter, Jerry shouted, "I love that formation! I love that formation!"

Thomas' touchdown proved to be the difference as the Bears—who trailed 14–0 at one point in the game—won 28–21.

Sharon Harrison
Sharon Davis Harrison worked for the Bears from 1984 through 1993. She died of a brain tumor on November 19, 2008. She was secretary to player personnel and community involvement. She was so good I dedicated my voice-mail message to her. If you called my office and no one answered, you would hear, "Hi, this is Pat McCaskey. I'm sorry that I can't take your call right now. Please leave a message with Sharon Davis; she is efficient and pleasant."

It was wonderful that the Bears won so many games during Sharon's tenure. It was also a highlight to come into Halas Hall in the morning and hear Sharon talking on the telephone with Leigh, who was in the Middle East while they were dating. She talked loudly as if she needed to shout all the way there. My wife Gretchen and I had the honor of attending their wedding in Christ Community Church in Zion. It was a wonderful celebration.

Sharon worked for the Bears until 1993. After she had left to be a full-time wife and mother, John Bostrom and I started the Sharon Harrison Award. Whenever we talked about a secretary who was efficient and pleasant, we said that she was worthy of the Sharon Harrison Award.

In the history of the Bears, there have been at least three great secretaries: my grandmother, Min Halas; my mother, Virginia McCaskey; and Leigh's wife, Sharon Harrison.

Chapter 8

A BEARS LOVE STORY

I am one of 11 children born to my mother, Virginia McCaskey, and my father, the late Edward McCaskey, who passed away in April 2003.

Mom is a member of the Chicago Bears board of directors and is its secretary. Michael, chairman of the board of directors, is the oldest of the 11. Tim, the team's vice president, is the second oldest, followed by Ellen and myself.

From there, it's Mary, Ned, Anne, George, Rich, Brian, and Joseph. Ned is a Bears board member, as is George, who also serves as the team's senior director of ticket operations. Rich is involved in the Bears' front office, while Brian is a board member and the Bears' senior director of business development.

My mom went to St. Hilary Grade School in Chicago, and graduated from St. Scholastica Academy High School. At Grandpa's insistence, Mom went off to college at Drexel Institute of Technology in Philadelphia, where Grandpa's brother, Walter, coached. She studied business because she wanted to be Grandpa's secretary in the Bears' office after graduation.

Dad, who at the time was attending the University of Pennsylvania, also located in Philadelphia, met Mom on a semi-blind date in 1941.

My mom and dad had to wait quite a while before finally getting married in 1943.

They dated as often as he could find her for about a six-week period, but he never attempted to kiss her. Mom thought she would break this romantic impasse, so one Sunday morning before Mass she grabbed him and kissed him!

Shortly after he had recovered from that assault, he said, "Let's get married."

"You're in a hurry, aren't you?" she replied.

However, the wedding wouldn't take place as quickly as either Mom or Dad would have wanted.

In 1942, Dad went to summer school and worked seven days a week. He worked the 3:00 PM to 11:00 PM shift in the Baltimore & Ohio freight yard at 24th and Wharton in Philadelphia and earned $43 a week. Dad was able to save a lot of money, and he bought Mom an engagement ring.

Mom begged Dad to show her the ring, but Dad thought otherwise. "No," he said. "Not until I get your father's okay." So Mom and Dad made a trip to Chicago to see Grandpa.

At around 4:00 in the afternoon, shortly after they arrived in Chicago, Grandpa roared into the apartment and said to Dad, "You wanted to see me?"

"Yes, sir," Dad said.

Grandpa said, "Come on in the bedroom."

There were two twin beds in the bedroom. Grandpa started taking his clothes off, right down to his underwear. The first air-conditioning unit my Dad had ever seen—Grandpa was one of the first to own one—was rattling and shaking. Grandpa lay down on one of the beds and asked, "Aren't you going to have a nap?"

Dad said, "Oh, yes sir." He took his outer clothes off and lay down on the other bed.

After a while Grandpa asked, "When do you want to talk to me? What's on your mind?"

Dad Learns His Rank

My father, Edward McCaskey, had a tour of duty with the army during World War II. For a period of time, he was stationed at Camp Rucker, Alabama, with the 66th Division, known as the Fighting Black Hens. Every 50 minutes, members of the 66th Division had to stop what they were doing and shout, "Ah, the Black Hens!"

Dad first arrived at Camp Rucker with an Irish setter after a long drive from Camp Blanding, Florida. He let the dog out. She ran, and as Dad was trying to catch her, he heard a voice say, "You'll never get that dog, lieutenant."

Dad looked over and saw an enlisted man leaning against a door jamb wearing a hat placed on the back of his head, his tie down, and his legs crossed. Dad said, "How dare you talk to me that way, soldier. You come to attention and salute."

The enlisted man said, "Ah, go get three more."

Dad asked, "What do you mean, 'Go get three more'?"

"Go get three more second lieutenants. I don't salute lieutenants unless they're first lieutenants, and second lieutenants have to be four of them," the enlisted man replied.

The enlisted man happened to be Phil Foster, who would later play Frank De Fazio on the television show *Laverne & Shirley*. Foster also appeared on such programs as *The Tonight Show Starring Johnny Carson*, *The Ed Sullivan Show*, and *The Love Boat*. Foster and Dad became great friends; in fact, Dad became a godfather to one of Foster's sons.

"Well, I want your permission to consider myself engaged to Virginia, and I bought a ring," Dad replied.

So Dad showed Grandpa the ring.

Grandpa asked, "How much did you pay for this?"

Dad said, "$155."

"Don't you know I have a jewelry store?" Grandpa said. "You'd have done much better than this. Okay. We'll go to the Edgewater Beach Hotel and you can give her the ring, but you can't get married."

"Yes, sir," was Dad's response.

Shortly thereafter, Mom and Dad went to dinner with Grandma and Grandpa. After a while Grandpa excused himself and said, "I've got some work to do." He stood up and shook Dad's hand. Dad looked, and there was $10 in his hand to pay for the dinner.

A little later, Mom and Dad went to listen to Shep Fields and his orchestra. The orchestra was accompanied by Ralph Young, who went on to become a big hit with Tony Sandler (Sandler sang in French, while Young sang in English). Then they went out on the beach along Lake Michigan, and Dad gave Mom the ring.

Now all Mom and Dad had to do was persuade Grandpa to give them permission to get married, but that wouldn't happen for a few more months. The United States was at war with Japan and Germany. Dad was in the ROTC at the University of Pennsylvania and would be going off to war soon; Grandpa ended up being stationed in Norman, Oklahoma, with the U.S. Navy.

However, Grandpa flew in to Washington on leave from Norman in order to see the Bears play the Redskins for the NFL championship on December 13, 1942. Mom and Dad saw this as a great opportunity to ask Grandpa for his permission to get married, so they decided to attend the game, as well.

The Bears trailed Washington late in the game. Dad looked over at Mom and saw that she was crying.

"What's the matter? Why are you crying? It's only a football game," he asked.

Mom said, "You don't think Dad will let us get married if the Bears lose, do you?"

The Bears fell to the Redskins 14–6, but after the game, Grandpa told Mom and Dad, "Yes, you can get married. It's all right."

Grandpa started giving orders to Grandma about getting the invitations printed, who to invite to the wedding, and where it should be held. So all of that was taken care of. Dad and Mom were to be married later in December. Mom's cousin, Carol Hutton, was going to be the maid of honor.

But just as quickly, the pending marriage hit another snag. The wedding ended up being called off because someone at the University of Pennsylvania told Walter Halas at Drexel that Dad had reportedly stolen money from the class treasury and was only marrying Mom for Grandpa's money.

Dad didn't know what to do. One morning he stopped over at Phil's Bar, a restaurant on campus that he frequented, to get a cup of tea and a doughnut before he hurried to his next class.

The owner of the restaurant knew Dad, and pointed to two gentlemen sitting nearby.

"Mac, two guys over there want to see you," he told Dad.

Both men were wearing double-breasted camel's hair coats and snap-brim hats. One of the gentlemen was puffing on a cigar, and Dad thought, *Uh-oh*.

Dad walked over and asked, "You gentlemen want to see me?"

One of them asked, "Well, are you McCaskey?"

Dad said, "Yes, I am."

One of the gentlemen looked up from his plate and said, "Well, I'm Bert Bell of the Philadelphia Eagles. This is Art Rooney of the Pittsburgh Steelers. [George] Halas sent us here to investigate you. I talked to Bill Lennox." (Lennox was in charge of all ticket sales at the University of Pennsylvania, which had been selling out every football game.)

Bell said, "Bill Lennox says you're okay. If you're okay with Bill Lennox, you're okay with me."

Then Art Rooney took the cigar out of his mouth and said, "If you're okay with Bert, you're okay with me. Whoever said Halas was an angel?"

Out they walked. It was enervating for Dad.

Dad finally got his name cleared of the charges by securing letters of support from prominent people in Philadelphia and Lancaster, his hometown. By this time, however, Grandpa was having second thoughts and decided that Mom and Dad should not be married until after the war was over.

Mom was frustrated, and so she called Dad and asked, "Don't you want to get married?"

"Yes, I do," Dad said, "but I have to respect your father's wishes."

"No, you don't," she insisted. "He'll never let us get married."

My mom and dad were happily married for 60 years.

Mom had a talk with Dad's mother, who was friends with some Catholic priests in Lancaster. One of those priests was Father Fitzgerald, whose classmate in seminary, Father Reed, had a little church in Bel Air, Maryland. They reached a decision that Mom would take a train on the Pennsylvania Railroad from Chicago to Philadelphia. From there, Mom and Dad would go to Bel Air and get married.

There was one hitch, however: Uncle Walter, who was home visiting, saw her at the train station in Chicago! So Mom and Dad had to make different plans. She took a train from Chicago on the Baltimore & Ohio Railroad to Baltimore, and Dad met her there. They went to a rooming house where my Dad's father lived. He was a construction electrician in a Baltimore shipyard, and got Mom and Dad each a room.

The next morning, February 2, 1943, Mom and Dad went to the Cathedral for Mass and Communion. When Mass concluded, they got on the bus, went to Bel Air, and visited the little church and rectory. Father Reed said, "I will marry you in the nuns' chapel."

The nuns' chapel was tiny; it had four pews and two windows. The matron of honor was Father Reed's cook. The best man was the cook's nephew.

After the ceremony, Mom and Dad went back to the rectory. Dad opened his wallet and asked, "What do I owe you, Father?"

Father Reed looked into the wallet. Dad had a $10 bill and a $1 bill. Father Reed didn't wait for Dad to pull out the money; he took the $10!

Go On Without Us

Before Super Bowl X between the Steelers and Cowboys took place on January 18, 1976, at the Orange Bowl in Miami, Florida, Dad sent this telegram to NFL commissioner Pete Rozelle:

"Son Joseph ill. Virginia and I unable to attend Super Bowl. Urge that you proceed with game as scheduled."

So Mom and Dad had one dollar as they started their lives together. They walked across the road to a restaurant and indulged in a wedding breakfast that consisted of ham with raisin sauce and mashed potatoes. Mom slipped Dad a half dollar under the table because the bill was $1.20. Dad left the waitress a generous tip of 30¢.

Chapter 9

GROWING UP IN A FOOTBALL FAMILY

My parents wove a pattern of hard work and discipline into the lives of their children. They stitched this pattern with love.

My mother always found it amusing when someone asked her how much hired help she had. That was probably the reason my father nicknamed her "Laughing Girl." She did all the cooking, laundry, and housework. The only time she got a real break was when she went into the hospital to have another baby.

During those interludes, Mrs. Passarelli, a family friend, took care of us. Instead of dinners featuring hamburgers or hot dogs, she prepared homemade pizza or spaghetti and meatballs. While waving a wooden spoon covered with meat sauce, she would yell, "You kids stop fighting." She never had to tell on us because my parents knew all too well about the tussles we got into.

There were many spats in our home, and my parents used belts, fly swatters, spatulas, and pizza paddles as instruments of discipline. While an addition was being built to our home in 1958, my brother, Tim, hid a pizza paddle and wouldn't tell my father where he hid it. When my

My mom and dad, Virginia and Ed McCaskey

father's discipline was deemed too severe, we buried one of his watches in the family vegetable garden.

The McCaskeys' idea of family planning was to have their children born during the Chicago Bears' off-seasons. Six brothers eventually shared a bedroom, with three sets of bunk beds and three sets of dresser drawers. Each brother had two and a half drawers. Each of us carved his initials into his drawers, but there were many disputes over the half-drawers.

Mike and Tim, my oldest brothers, lulled us to sleep at night with their discussions, which usually centered around whatever sport happened to be in season. If it was baseball season, for instance, they would debate whether Luis Aparicio of the White Sox or Ernie Banks of the Cubs was the better shortstop.

But no matter what the season, whenever my father brought my mother home with a new baby, we stopped playing football in the side yard after he parked the car, got out, and shouted, "Boys, get over here and say hello to your mother and your new brother (or sister)." A simple long jump over some bushes behind our west end zone put us a short sprint away from the car.

We shouted, "First one there gets to see the baby first!"

Whoever got there first received more instructions from my father. "Give your mother a kiss," he'd say.

"Aw, Ma, what would the guys say?" the boy who got there first would ask (after all, no boy ever wanted anyone to see him actually kissing his mother).

My mother said, "Don't you 'Aw, Ma' me."

Each of us kissed my mother, greeted the baby, leaped back over the bushes, and resumed playing football. The halftime break was finished.

When it came to football, we were like children who received a parlor game for Christmas. Our motto was, "Let's get started; we can learn the rules later."

After the game, my older brothers quizzed the younger ones on the fundamentals.

"How many points for a touchdown?"

"Six."

"How many points for a field goal?"

"Three."

"How many points for a safety?"

"Two."

"How many points for a kick after a touchdown?"

"One."

My father was a hardworking man who taught all of his children right from wrong.

"How many points for a kick after a field goal?"

"One."

"Wrong. There is no such thing as a point after a field goal."

"Check."

Many of us eventually went on to play organized football. As football players, we recognized our responsibility to the community that supported our games. We participated in many civic functions; we were Cub Scouts and then Boy Scouts; we were altar boys and then patrol boys.

Education was very important in our home, and chores were an essential part of our upbringing. Grass had to be mowed, snow had to be shoveled, dog pens had to be cleaned, and vegetable gardens had to be cultivated.

My father didn't just give us our marching orders; he led by example. He worked harder than any of his sons, and he had a great sense of humor, especially when he happened to be cultivating the vegetable garden with a pitchfork and found one of his watches!

All of us were raised with discipline and love. Each of us was special in the eyes of Laughing Girl and Big Ed.

Naming Rights

A few years after World War II, Max Kendrick, who had served in the army with my dad, told him, "Ed, all of your troubles with your father-in-law will be over if you just name your next son after him." My father replied, "Nothing doing." Shortly after my birth, my father sent Kendrick a small baby trophy with the name Patrick Kendrick McCaskey on it.

My father was so stubborn that he named his next son after himself: Edward William McCaskey. Finally, the next son was named George Halas McCaskey. That was in 1956, the year the Bears began their quest for a new stadium.

———

On many childhood Sundays, it didn't matter what time we got up, as long as we were ready to leave at 7:45 AM. After all, Mass started at 8:00, and it wouldn't do anybody any good to miss a golden moment. In order to meet this first of many deadlines on those glorious days, my mother was on everybody's back to get up and get going. Through the grace of God, no doubt, my seven brothers, my three sisters, my parents, and I managed to pile into both family cars and get to church on time.

At one point in the ceremony, Father Patrick Bird asked the congregation to pause and recall their sins. (I smiled as I remembered mine.) Filled with the spirit of the Lord, the parishioners would file out of the church after Mass had ended and fight to be the first out of the parking lot. (You can tell we are Christians by our love.) Inevitably, the car that I was riding in had to be stopped three times for peace negotiations during the three-mile ride home. Fights over the comics and sports sections of the Chicago newspapers were predictably high. Eventually, our family would make it home safely, and we counted our blessings.

The preparations would then begin for the exodus to Wrigley Field where the Chicago Bears played their home games. Everyone tried to get breakfast in the kitchen at the same time. The boys fought to use the toaster. The girls were busy making hot chocolate and sandwiches. My mother was busy getting breakfast for my father, Big Ed. He would be reading the sports sections.

All of this had to be accomplished with a minimum of wasted motion. As Laughing Girl always pointed out, we had to leave the house by 11:00 AM. It was imperative for us to be at the stadium by noon, one hour before the game started. Boots, thermal underwear, gloves, stocking caps, overcoats, blankets, and binoculars all had to be rationed out equally among the 13 members of our family and then loaded into the cars.

With God on our side, the hourlong journey passed safely as we prayed the family rosary and offered it for a Bears victory. Between the start of the game at 1:05 PM and the final gun at approximately 4:00, there passed my father's outrage at bad officiating, my mother's tears, and my unsuccessful attempts to escape from the whole scene. After the game, the fearsome foursome—my four youngest brothers—scurried through the seats to pick up the beer-soaked game programs. The older youngsters snorted at them until Big Ed and Laughing Girl reminded

Me, my brother Tim, the Bears' mascot, and my brother Mike take in a game at Wrigley Field.

the old-timers how silly they looked doing the same thing a few seasons before. Then we stood outside the locker room to get a closer look at our gladiators, especially Bill George, the Bears' middle linebacker and Bill Wade, the Bears' quarterback.

The car radio would play the game's highlights and broke up the monotony of the trip back home. Traffic on the highway was usually very congested; occasionally a Studebaker blitz cut our car off, but Big Ed would calmly call an audible and option into another lane. We managed to arrive home in time for a 6:00 PM dinner. My father would finish the grace with a special plea for the Lord to "please convert the Russians." The prayers ended just in time for the 6:15 sports broadcast on WGN radio. While we feasted on mutton and goblets of real milk, we heard the scores from across the nation.

After dinner one of the younger boys was sent to buy the latest Chicago newspapers. They presented an in-depth focus and special interviews with the opposing coaches and players. It took a long time for the papers to make their way around to all the members of the family. More than one but less than 14 bowls of ice cream would be spilled in the process. If you were the last to read them, you had to speed-read to finish before the 10:00 PM news begins. Two couches comprised the seven box seats in the television room. Three kitchen chairs were shuffled in to make up the grandstand. Standing-room-only passes were issued to the last three people to read the newspapers.

Channel 9 was the first station that was tuned in because it was the first station that presented the sports. The news was over by 10:30, which coincided with the family curfew. Big Ed then called the final play of the day: "Go right up the hill. Brush your teeth and say your prayers."

———

When Grandpa coached the Bears, his players had to start training camp by running the "Halas Mile." Each player was timed running the mile—

four laps around the St. Joseph College track. Players had to run the mile within a certain time frame, which was different for linemen, running backs, and so on. That's how I got interested in running.

But in the summer of 1966, I was interested in having a good season on the gridiron because it was my senior year at Notre Dame High School in Niles, Illinois (I missed nearly all of my junior year because of a hernia). So in preparation for the upcoming season, I ran five miles and threw 200 passes per day.

And who better to train with than NFL players? After two-a-day practices at the Bears' training camp, Bill Wade took the time to tutor me in the fundamentals of quarterbacking. Before each session, he reached down to the ground and looked for a four-leaf clover, believing that meant we would have a good workout. He'd tell me, "Everyone I've ever tutored in quarterbacking became an All-American." That was certainly a confidence builder!

After the workouts, my younger brothers, Ned and George, Ken Powers—a high school teammate—and I sought relief in a nearby quarry that was full of water. I didn't want my brothers to venture too far from Ken and me, so we warned them to watch out for "Gator Man," who, if he caught them, could gobble them up in one bite.

One afternoon, while floating on a raft in the quarry, I heard Ned cry out, "Pat, I think I'm in quicksand!" So I paddled over to him and helped him get on the raft. (I guess I saved his life.)

Growing boys that we were, we never missed a meal at training camp. We gobbled down plenty of good food. I always got a laugh out of Ken's table manners. Before he would eat a piece of cake, he said, "Hi, cake. I'm going to eat you."

Training with the Bears in Rensselaer paid dividends. At the start of August football practice at Notre Dame, I won the 600-yard run in 1:21.8. I finished 100 yards ahead of everyone else in my heat. Al Loboy, the defensive coordinator, was so impressed that he made me a linebacker. He also gave me the responsibility of calling defensive signals.

That's me, playing quarterback and running the mile for Notre Dame High School.

Notre Dame's head coach, Fran Willett, also rewarded me by giving me one of the 11 sets of brand-new protective shoulder pads. In addition, I received a helmet with a birdcage facemask. Although I also played quarterback, I didn't find it necessary to change over to light shoulder pads and the single-bar facemask that quarterbacks wore in those days. I was a linebacker!

Willett's drills were unique; four defensive linemen went up against 11 offensive players, then the four linebackers took their turn going against the offense.

While I was playing quarterback during one practice, Denny Conway, the backfield coach, told me to throw my passes with the nose of the football down. I insisted that the nose of the football should be up. He asked me who taught me that. As quietly and respectfully as I could, I replied, "Bill Wade." Coach Conway gave way and allowed me to throw the way Wade had taught me.

A good friend of mine on the team, Owen Bauler, started on defense and played on special teams, like I did. But we both had a burning desire to play offense, too. After practices, we sat on the west steps behind the school, commiserated, and encouraged each other.

For a period of time after training camp broke at St. Joseph's College, the Bears practiced and held team meetings at Notre Dame High School while they waited for the Cubs to finish their season at Wrigley Field. We saw the Bears walking around the building, and sometimes I spotted Grandpa. That was quite a thrill.

About a week before our first game, I happened to get kicked in the left shin during practice. I went to the hospital and had it examined. The doctor gave me clearance to play, but I had to wear a hard pad over the injured area. So I had to shave my left shin and tape the hard pad on before every game.

Prior to the first game, we got to choose our uniform numbers. Bill Casey, our offensive coordinator, told me, "You're starting at linebacker, but you'll be playing a lot of quarterback before the season is over. As a senior, you get first choice of the quarterback numbers." I chose No. 10 because that had been Rick Gorzynski's number. Gorzynski played quarterback and safety, and was the kicker and punter on the 1961 team that went undefeated (10–0). He was also a great baseball player.

On Friday, September 16, Notre Dame hosted Taft and we won handily 42–19. Tom Newton got us going in the first quarter by breaking off a 52-yard touchdown run. Steve Hurley kicked the extra point—one of several extra points he converted during the evening.

Newton went on to score another touchdown in the third quarter on a two-yard run, while Owen Bauler added touchdown runs of one and 19 yards.

Meanwhile, Greg Luzinski—yes, this is the same Greg Luzinski who enjoyed a long major league career with the Philadelphia Phillies and Chicago White Sox and hit 307 career home runs—scored a one-yard touchdown run in the second quarter.

Right before halftime, the Taft quarterback dropped back to pass. My assignment was to cover the running back on the right side, but he stayed in to block. So I darted past him, sacked the quarterback, and forced him to fumble the ball away.

With the game out of reach in the fourth quarter, I took over at quarterback. I immediately called a spread formation and a pass play, but threw an incompletion. Coach Willett promptly yanked me from the game. He didn't want me to show any of our fancy formations to future opponents.

With 7:30 left in the game, our second-team defense took the field, and I went to the sideline. Taft completed a pass, and the receiver who caught the ball was making his way to the end zone. I waited until the officials weren't looking, then I ran onto the field, and tried to run down the receiver! But I was too late; the Taft receiver scored.

At the end of our next offensive series, I assumed our reserves had entered the game, but I was wrong. Our starting punting unit actually took the field, and I was supposed to be the blocking back. In a team film session the following week, Jack Cole, the special teams coach, bellowed, "You should have come off the bench on that play, McCaskey!"

The following Friday, we played host to Lane. We battled Lane to a scoreless tie during the first half. At intermission, we didn't go to the locker room for some reason. Instead, we gathered under the scoreboard at the south end of our field. "You have the chance to be one of the best Notre Dame teams," Coach Willett told us. "The second half will be remembered for many years to come."

That little pep talk got us going. Steve Hurley put us on the scoreboard and gave us a 3–0 lead after he booted a 20-yard field goal.

In the fourth quarter, Owen Bauler caught a punt and took advantage of a huge block by Frank Urban, who took out two Lane players with one block. Owen then got behind a wall of Notre Dame blockers for a 64-yard punt return down the east sideline. Lane finally knocked him out of bounds at its 1-yard line. On second down, Greg Luzinski took it up the middle for a touchdown. We walked off with a 9–0 victory.

Despite doing well in passing drills during practice the following week, I didn't get an opportunity to quarterback the first team, so I pouted. But the next day, Coach Casey apologized to me because he didn't have enough time to tell Coach Willett about my progress. However, Coach Casey also made it clear that if I ever exhibited my displeasure like that again, I'd be kicked off the team.

"Do you think you're the best quarterback we have?" Coach Willett asked me.

I cleverly replied, "Yes."

"I know what you're worried about—getting a scholarship to college," he said. "[But] I've got your school all picked out for you. A good friend

The Bull

Had Greg Luzinski been a Chicago Bear instead of a Major League Baseball player, he and Walter Payton might have made a potent running back tandem. I know both of them in ways that most people do not.

Luzinski and I were football teammates at Notre Dame High School in Niles. After practices, Luzinski and his parents gave me a ride home to Des Plaines. Then they proceeded to their home in Prospect Heights.

Luzinski played fullback, inside linebacker, and was the punter. I played quarterback, outside linebacker, and blocking back on punts. He weighed 205 pounds, yet was one of the fastest players on the squad. I weighed 180 pounds and usually led the team when we had to run laps.

I often faked to Luzinski off tackle, and he drew quite a crowd. Then it was easy to slip around end or throw to halfback Mike Newton in the flat. (When we got near the goal line, I gave it to the one who was the most deserving!) Anybody could have quarterbacked with Luzinski (who led the team in scoring) at fullback...and several of us did.

Fran Willett, our head coach and a member of the Illinois High School Coaches Hall of Fame, said Luzinski "had a lot of offers for football. Everybody wanted him. He had a lot of talent. God gave him everything. He could have been a champion swimmer and a hockey player. He was a money player inside the 10 [-yard line]. We wouldn't allow the kid to lift weights. He was strong as a freshman and we were afraid he would get muscle-bound. He was a fine punter; his hang time was real good. The opponents only averaged 0.3 yards on returns. He was real coachable, had good quickness, and was a fine pass receiver. He could have played any position: guard, tight end. You'll never lose with kids like him."

One of the many coaches to offer Luzinski a college football scholarship was Dan Devine, then the head coach at Missouri. At the dinner to honor all the all-conference players in Illinois, Devine said to Luzinski, "Even though you're only a junior, I'm offering you a full four-year football scholarship."

But after he had graduated from high school, Luzinski chose baseball, signing with the Philadelphia Phillies. Eventually he also gained fame as a member of the 1983 "Winning Ugly" Chicago White Sox. Had Luzinski chosen football, his first year of eligibility for play in the National Football League would have been 1972.

of mine, Jim LaRue, is the head coach at Arizona. I'll explain to him how we needed you to call the signals on defense."

Well, I was a normal Catholic boy. And I wanted to play quarterback for the University of Notre Dame, which was named after God's mother, Mary. But for now, I had to concentrate on the season ahead.

On September 30, Marian Central came to Notre Dame, and we won 54–13.

Luzinski was nicknamed "the Bull" during his major league playing days due to his strong, stocky build. He bulled over Marian Central this particular day, scoring on runs of two and three yards. He also intercepted a pass and returned it 45 yards for a score.

Meanwhile, Bill Harrington galloped 82 yards for a touchdown and tacked on an additional touchdown on a 36-yard run. Bauler also got into the act, taking the ball into the end zone from one and two yards out. Hurley was automatic on point-after kicks, converting six.

In the fourth quarter, I took the reins at quarterback. On one play, I faked a handoff to the fullback at right tackle, rolled right on a belly option-8 pass, and ran nine yards for a touchdown.

What a game!

We took to the road on October 8 and visited Carmel for its homecoming. This would be a much closer contest than the game we enjoyed the previous week.

Bob Rammon put us up 7–0 in the first quarter when he intercepted a pass and returned it 46 yards for a touchdown and Steve Hurley kicked the extra point.

In the second quarter, Carmel got back into the game with an 80-yard touchdown run that, unfortunately, ran around my side. However, Hurley kicked a 30-yard field goal to give us a 10–7 lead.

At halftime, Coach Cole reminded us that we were ahead. I made up my mind to quit feeling sorry for myself because I wasn't starting at quarterback and resolved to do my best at linebacker.

In the fourth quarter, Greg Luzinski gave us some cushion by scoring a two-yard touchdown. Carmel marched 60 yards on its ensuing possession, but I knocked down a pass during the drive. Linebacker Kevin Murningham then sealed our victory by picking off a pass with one minute remaining in the contest.

We spoiled Carmel's homecoming by winning 17–7.

Our own homecoming game was on tap next. In the week preceding the game, I found out that I had been taken off special teams, which upset me until linebacker Joe Petricca told me, "Maybe you're gonna play more quarterback."

We took the field against St. Francis on October 14 and recorded a 34–6 victory to make our homecoming a happy one. Greg Luzinski and the Newtons, Mike and Tom, carried the load for us offensively. Luzinski and Mike scored on runs of one and 20 yards, respectively, while Hurley kicked the extra points. In the second quarter, Luzinski added an eight-yard touchdown run.

Pete Newell's 38-yard interception return for a touchdown put us comfortably ahead in the third quarter. Tom Newton wrapped up our scoring for the night with a three-yard touchdown run.

By the way, Petricca's prediction was correct. I did get to play some quarterback in the second half.

Our season continued on Friday, October 21, as we played host to Elgin St. Edward. Our backfield was decimated going into the game—Tom Newton, Owen Bauler, and Gary Aylesworth were all hurt—so we had to pass more. Their injuries enabled me to step in and get my chance at quarterback. It was a cold and windy night; we had the wind at our back in the first and third quarters, but had to face it during the second and fourth quarters.

During one offensive series in the first quarter, we ran a belly option-8 pass with Greg Luzinski at fullback and Mike Newton the near back right. I faked to Greg off our right tackle, Jerry Jasinski, then threw an 11-yard touchdown pass to Mike.

At the end of our next series, we again ran a belly option-8 pass. Once again, I faked to Luzinski off right tackle, rolled right, and this time threw a 19-yard touchdown pass to Mike.

In the third quarter, we ran the play a third time successfully. This time, Mike was on the receiving end of a 43-yard touchdown pass.

This play finally failed, so it was decided to alter things a bit during an offensive series later in the game. Our coaches told us to run the belly option-8 pass like we normally did, but this time I would run the ball. So I faked to Luzinski, rolled right, faked a pass to Mike Newton, and ran 24 yards for a touchdown.

Mike also contributed another touchdown on a 12-yard run, while Bob Rammon blocked a punt that Luzinski recovered and ran in for a three-yard touchdown. Mark Havlis wrapped things up by tallying an 18-yard touchdown run.

Steve Hurley nailed seven extra-point kicks during the game, and my debut at quarterback was a successful one as we defeated St. Edward 49–7.

Our next game was held on a Sunday (October 30) at Holy Cross. And for the second straight week, we won going away, this time 54–16.

Yours truly continued to run the offense at quarterback. I enjoyed one of my most productive games this particular Sunday, throwing a nine-yard touchdown pass to Frank Urban in the first quarter and a seven-yard strike to Owen Bauler in the second. In addition, I capped off another scoring drive in the second quarter with a two-yard quarterback sneak.

This latter drive began when Mike Newton—who had a brilliant game—returned a kickoff 47 yards. Newton also returned the opening kickoff 75 yards for a touchdown. Then in the second half, he took part in a razzle-dazzle play where he caught the kickoff and handed the ball off to Kevin Host, who broke loose for a 96-yard touchdown.

Bill Harrington took over for me at quarterback in the fourth quarter, and he didn't miss a beat. He tossed touchdown passes of 20 yards to John Ellefson and 27 yards to Ken Powers. Powers scored again during the quarter when he blocked a punt, recovered it, and ran it into the end zone.

Once again, Steve Hurley provided steady kicking as he was successful on seven extra-point chances.

Despite throwing two touchdown passes, Coach Willett wasn't pleased with the fact that I also threw three interceptions.

The morning after the game, right defensive end Rick Rammon talked to me before sociology class started. He said, "We were a running team on offense until you started at quarterback. After you had the three interceptions yesterday, Coach Willett fumed on the sideline. I think you'll start the next game, though."

"I hope so," I replied.

Rick Rammon was right. Coach Willett kept me in as the team's starting quarterback, and I made sure I didn't let him or the team down. We rolled to a 45–0 victory at Marmion on November 4.

In the first quarter, Greg Luzinski scored on a four-yard touchdown run, while Steve Hurley kicked the extra point.

I completed a 12-yard pass to Mike Newton during our first scoring drive, and also scrambled for a good gain. However, I got hit hard on one play and started to limp a bit. Coach Cole asked me if I was all right and I said yes. Even so, Bill Harrington took over for me at quarterback and ended up scoring on a five-yard run to complete another offensive drive.

I told Coach Cole that I was fine and I wanted to get back in the game. He said, "Look at that scoreboard. We're way ahead. All right, you want to get back in the game? You can run down kickoffs."

So I did. Hurley kicked off near the end of the first quarter, and I helped run it down.

I did get to run one play at quarterback in the second quarter—our old, reliable belly option-8 pass. I faked to Greg Luzinski, then ran to the right because our receivers were covered. We did get some points out of the drive as Hurley kicked a field goal.

At halftime, we all sat in the bus that brought us to the game. Before Coach Willett started his halftime talk, I looked out the window; the gray sky, to me, looked very dismal. Coach Willett told me in front of the team, "McCaskey, there's a time to throw the ball, and I'll let you know when that time is."

"Yes, sir," I replied.

"You'll start the second half at quarterback."

"Yes, sir."

I looked out the bus window again, and wouldn't you know it? The gray sky looked great!

In the third quarter, Luzinski rumbled 74 yards for a touchdown. Later, Coach Willett determined it was time to go to the air, and I was eager to do my part. I dropped back and threw a 16-yard touchdown pass to Frank Urban.

Mike Newton had a 27-yard interception return for a touchdown, while Mark Havlis added a six-yard touchdown run to complete the night's scoring.

Late in the fourth quarter, Coach Willett sent me in at left halfback with an improvised play: a power sweep pass. I took the pitchout, shook off a tackler, and threw the ball as far as I could...for an interception.

Our season finale—and my last game as a high school player—took place on Friday, November 11. We ended the season by knocking off St. Procopius at home 37–12.

I capped off my prep career with a one-yard quarterback sneak for a touchdown, but this game belonged to Greg Luzinski. First, he tackled the St. Procopius punter in the end zone for a safety. Then he scored on a one-yard run. In the fourth quarter, he caught an 83-yard touchdown pass from Harrington. Earlier in the game, Harrington hooked up with Gary Aylesworth for a 19-yard score. Kevin Host added a long 76-yard touchdown run.

Overall, we enjoyed a dream season. Our team finished 9–0, outscored our opponents 341–80, and was ranked as one of the top prep teams in the country. We won each game by an average of 29 points.

It took a lot of practice and patience to become the starting quarterback at Notre Dame High School.

———

After the regular season, the seniors and the freshmen were scheduled to play the juniors and the sophomores. The juniors and the sophomores practiced diligently the week before the game, but their hard work didn't impress the seniors, who constantly made fun of them.

The game took place a week later. Coach Willett coached the seniors and the freshmen. Before the game, he told me, "You can pass as much as you want."

I thought, *I'll show him. We'll run it every play.*

I admittedly got very angry after the juniors and the sophomores scored first. I hollered at my teammates in the huddle to take the game seriously or we wouldn't win. Center Mike Shaw reassured me by saying, "Don't worry about it. We're going to win."

I apologized, then I called a wedge blocking play over right guard Bill Marquardt. Right halfback Mike Newton and fullback Ken Powers would share duties carrying the ball. When Marquardt got tired, I called a wedge blocking play over left guard Dick Ryglowski.

My concerns were all for naught. Powers scored on touchdown runs in both the first and second quarters. Then in the third quarter, I called a belly option-8. I faked to Powers off right tackle Jerry Jasinski, and kept it around right end for a touchdown. The seniors and the freshmen won the game handily 21–7.

A few days later, I was in Al Loboy's first-period sociology class when the announcement came over the public address system that Bob Feltz (safety), Greg Luzinski (fullback), Pete Newell (defensive tackle), Ken Powers (linebacker), Rick Rammon (defensive end), Frank Urban (offensive end), and Pat McCaskey (quarterback) made the all-conference team. I was very surprised and happy because I had no idea that I was going to get any award.

After class, Coach Loboy congratulated Rick Rammon and me. I told him that I thought I hadn't played enough to deserve the honor.

My Brother Mike

When I was in second grade at St. Mary's School in Des Plaines, Illinois, I was in Sister Amata's class. My brother, Mike, was going from St. Mary's to Quigley Preparatory Seminary. I said to Sister Amata, "There isn't enough paper to write all the good things about my brother Mike."

At the end of the school year, Sister Amata gave me a stack of paper about a foot high. On the top of the stack was a note from her. On the top of the note were the initials "J.M.J." These stood for Jesus, Mary, and Joseph. She had also written, "Here is some paper to get you started on writing about your brother Mike."

Fast-forward to the summer of 1964. I was going to be a sophomore at Notre Dame High School, and Mike was going to be a

My brother Mike and I

senior at Yale. I wanted to be a quarterback, and Mike wanted to be a receiver. So we worked out together.

At one point, I called for Mike to run a two-yard square-out. After the play went for an incompletion, he said to me, "You're calling out the signals in a clear, loud voice, but no receiver in the world can catch a two-yard square out when you throw it that hard."

In the summer of 1967, I had to give up playing football because of severe eye problems. I quietly put my newspaper clippings and trophies in the garbage. Mike and my mother later retrieved them.

When I got married in 1984, Mike served as my best man. When my son James was baptized in 1991, Mike was the godfather.

In 1985—the season the Bears went on to win the Super Bowl—Mike was named NFL Executive of the Year. In March 1997, the Bears moved into the new Halas Hall, a project Mike spearheaded.

When Mike went from president of the Bears to chairman, I remembered what my grandfather said to me in 1974. I had asked him how things were going with Jim Finks as the executive vice president and general manager of the Bears. My uncle Mugs had gone from president and general manager to president.

My grandfather said to me, "I'm delighted that Jim Finks is here. I've got my son back."

Likewise, Mike's move from president to chairman was an opportunity for me to get my brother back.

However, Coach Loboy said that Coach Willett spoke up for me at the all-conference selection meeting.

———

I had my heart set on playing football at the University of Notre Dame, but on the advice of Notre Dame assistant football coach Joe Yonto, I enrolled at Cheshire Academy in Connecticut to get another year of playing experience. Coach Yonto said that if I played well at Cheshire, then Notre Dame would seriously consider me for a scholarship.

He also wrote a letter about me to Steve Kuk, Cheshire's varsity football coach. Coach Kuk later told me that he designed a pro-style offense with me passing often for Cheshire based on Coach Yonto's letter.

However, while playing catcher on an area baseball team that summer, I developed noticeable eye problems, which caused me to allow a lot of passed balls. When my father asked me what the problem was, I said, "I can't follow the ball."

In late August, my eye doctor, George Jessen, asked me how much my football career meant to me.

I said, "It means a lot to me."

"Does it mean so much to you that you'd risk losing your sight?"

"No," I admitted.

I was diagnosed with keratoconus, a degenerative eye disorder that causes the cornea to thin. The cornea then changes shape from a normal curve to a more conelike appearance, which causes distortion of vision.

I remember Dad telling me, "The steel of manhood is tempered in the fire of adversity. Everybody has something wrong with them. Everyone's handicap is different because each of us is unique. When we are strong in an area in which others are weak, we are our brother's keeper."

I'm glad this is so, because many people have helped me over the years.

One day, I spoke with Grandpa about having to give up playing football. He told me how he started out in baseball but had to give that up because of a hip injury. It was only because of the baseball injury, he said, that he turned to football full time.

"It doesn't matter what you do, as long as you excel," he said.

Getting the news that I couldn't play football anymore took place just a short time before I left for Cheshire. I was beginning to feel like Marlon Brando's character in the movie *On the Waterfront*, when he said, "I coulda been a contender."

But when I arrived at Cheshire, an incident occurred that got me out of this mind-set.

I happened to be standing in line at the bookstore one day before classes began. I overheard one student say to another student, "We were going to have a great football team, but the quarterback had to give up football."

Then the other student asked, "What's his name?"

I fully expected to hear my name. But the first student replied, "Jeb Swift; he hurt his knee."

With football no longer an option, I went to college after prep school. I had my SAT scores sent to Indiana University, Miami of Ohio, and Ohio State. I was all set to go to Ohio State because that's the school James Thurber—a famous writer and cartoonist—attended. However, Dr. Jessen persuaded me to attend Indiana because his son Mike had gone there.

So I went to Indiana and began classes there in the fall of 1968. I then decided to try out for the cross country team, which had an A team and a B team. At the beginning of the season, I happened to be the worst runner on the B team, but by the end of the year, I worked my way up to become the B team's best runner. The highlight of the season for me was running four miles under 22 minutes at a meet held at the University of Chicago.

After the season, however, I had to give up running altogether due to my recurring eye problems, coupled with allergies. But Grandpa kept after me and insisted I seek medical solutions. He urged me to remain optimistic and to continue trying to improve myself.

Ten years passed, but thanks to "Dr. Halas," I was able to start running again in the summer of 1978.

While I was never a professional athlete, I more than held my own against pro football players when it came to running. In 1981, the Bears

Chris Evert

Chris Evert and I had a couple of innocent conversations in February of 1975, but there has been no communication between us since then. (At the risk of appearing falsely modest, she probably doesn't even remember me.)

Evert—the world's top-ranked player for a handful of years from the mid-1970s through the early 1980s—came to Chicago for a Virginia Slims Tournament being held at the International Amphitheater. I called legendary columnist Irv Kupcinet of the *Chicago Sun-Times* to ask for help in trying to meet her.

I didn't kid myself. I knew Kupcinet took my call for help because I was named after St. Patrick, who was the patron saint of public relations at the time for the Bears. (He was later named the patron saint of community involvement.)

"I would appreciate your help. I'd like to meet Chris Evert," I said.

He chuckled and then replied, "Let me call Ralph Leo, the public relations man at the Amphitheater."

He did, and Leo called me with the great news that he would arrange for a press pass for me. Then he asked, "Isn't she going with Jimmy Connors?"

I replied, "They broke up. Besides, I think she'd be better off with me."

"Spoken like a young man," he said.

When I asked my father for permission to borrow his car, he wanted to know why. After I had told him, he said, "I guess you feel pretty proud of yourself for arranging this without my help."

"There is some measure of self-esteem involved," I replied.

Before I left the office to go to the tournament, I received a lot of well wishes and offers of, well, assistance. Grandpa said, "Tell her I think she's great." Uncle Mugs said that I could stay overnight at his downtown Chicago bachelor apartment. Jim Finks pointed out that she gets approached from all sorts of people. He advised me to act as if I was just writing an article on a top athlete.

After her match, I made my pitch to Evert…and she seemed annoyed! The next day I gave her a copy of humorist James Thurber's fable, *The Little Girl and The Wolf*, for Valentine's Day. It's about the little girl who "took an automatic out of her basket and shot the wolf

160

dead." Moral of the story: it's not so easy to fool little girls nowadays as it used to be.

After her next match, I asked her if she had received it. "Yes, thanks, it was nice," she said.

And that was the extent of our relationship. Years later, I met my wife, who was cocaptain of the 1973 Wheaton College undefeated and untied women's tennis team. Both women are great champions, but my wife and I agree Evert is a better tennis player.

Tennis has been very good to my family in other ways too. Many years ago, my mother won the National Football League Wives Tournament. My brother Mike met his wife Nancy on the tennis courts at Harvard.

held a half-mile run to start training camp. Only one player, Kris Haines, finished ahead of me.

Next summer, the distance increased to a mile and a half, but I finished first. "I tried to stay with you," Walter Payton told me afterward. When Walter—who always took pride in keeping himself in top physical condition—told me that, it made all my running worthwhile.

My father kept after me to get corneal transplants. So in April 2003, I underwent a successful right corneal transplant. Ten months later, I had a successful left corneal transplant. After those two corneal transplants, along with two cataract surgeries, my eyes are fine now.

Chapter 10

SAYING GOOD-BYE TO A BELOVED BEAR

When George Halas died on Monday, October 31, 1983, I lost a grandfather, my godfather, and a great friend.

My earliest memories of Grandpa were of family gatherings. Toward the end of these evenings, he would give each of his grandchildren $5—which my mom promptly collected for our savings accounts.

One time, when I was about five years old, I asked him, "Grandpa, can I have the money now?"

My parents were very embarrassed, but he laughed with great appreciation. At the next gathering, I tried to put some money in his pockets. He liked that, too.

I started going to Bears games when I was five. My brothers and I sat on an army blanket next to the Bears' bench while Grandpa coached. After the games, we waited for him outside the Bears' locker room. Regardless of the outcome of the game, he said to each of us, "Hi, pal, how about a kiss for grandpa?"

Sometimes I was allowed to accompany my grandfather to the Pink Poodle press room in Wrigley Field where he met with reporters after the games. Once, after he had let out a string of profanities following a particularly painful loss, he remembered that I was sitting next to him. Then he said, "Now, fellas, all of that was off the record."

I started going to the Bears' training camps when I was seven. George Blanda taught us how to place-kick. Bill George taught us how to play linebacker. Bill Wade taught us how to play quarterback.

One year, I went to the camp at St. Joseph's College in Rensselaer, Indiana, with my brother Ned, my brother George, and my high school

My grandpa retired as head coach of the Bears in 1968.

football teammate, Ken Powers. At the start of the visit, Grandpa called us over to his golf cart after practice. He gave us some pocket money. When tight end Mike Ditka observed the transaction, he came over to participate.

Mike asked, "Hey, Coach, how about some of that for me?"

Grandpa replied, "Never mind."

Frequently, Grandpa and I ate dinner together after work. When a Bears fan would stop by our table to ask for an autograph, he would always comply. He loved the Bears and appreciated any sign that a fan did, too.

During one dinner at the Arizona Biltmore in the spring of 1975, Grandpa and I were sitting next to John MacLeod, then the head coach of the NBA's Phoenix Suns. When John began choking on some food, Grandpa leaped up from our table, applied the Heimlich maneuver, saved John's life, and then sat down as if nothing out of the ordinary had taken place.

For family dinners, I often drove him out to my parents' home in Des Plaines. He asked me about my girlfriends, and I asked him about his. We had no conflicts because he "never dated anyone under 48."

In February 1977, Grandpa sent me a wonderful note: "Long ago I determined that work exceeds talent. Work every day by writing every day. Make me even more proud than I am of you. Love, George."

During the last five years of Grandpa's life, his grandchildren took him out to dinner on his birthday. On February 2, 1983, his 88th birthday, we should have known that something was amiss because he told us that he did not swear anymore. He also said, "May the good Lord grant all of you as long and as wonderful a life as I have had."

He wanted me to call him George, but I felt uncomfortable. Mom was very much against it. So I went back to calling him Grandpa.

As busy as he was, he knew the value of daily exercise. His motivational slogan was, "Never go to bed a loser."

My grandfather, surrounded by his loving family

Grandpa died while I was on the way to Los Angeles for a Bears game against the Rams. I decided to proceed with my work the way Grandpa would have wanted. I worked the press breakfast the next morning and flew to Chicago for the wake and the funeral.

The wake could have been a very sad occasion, but thankfully so many people came up to my mother and the family to say they were fans and had to come to honor Grandpa. Several brought along personal letters from Grandpa or recalled a brief meeting many years before. The wake became a celebration of an extraordinarily rich and full life. Before the casket was closed, my brother Joseph said, "Good-bye, pal."

The funeral took place at St. Ita's Church in Chicago. My brothers Mike, Tim, Ned, Rich, Brian, and I were pallbearers. I read from

Lamentations and the Psalms to the congregation, and my brother George read from Paul's Letter to Timothy. In his homily, Father Banet, the president of St. Joseph's College, described George Halas as "a man of faith and a man of prayer." And he was.

After the funeral, my brother Mike found a letter Grandpa had written to Uncle Mugs. Dated June 12, 1945, the letter was written aboard a ship "somewhere off the Philippines" when Grandpa was in the navy during World War II.

At the time, Mugs was in a Naval Cadet training program. Grandpa wrote of his pride in Mugs' accomplishments, encouraging him to keep making his best efforts. Mugs was thinking of switching from engineering (Grandpa's college major) to business. Grandpa wrote, "Dear pal...it always has been my thought that regardless of what you received your

Grandpa Serves His Country

Grandpa served in the navy during World War II. Initially, he served at a base in Norman, Oklahoma, and then became a Welfare and Recreation Officer for the Seventh Fleet in the South Pacific. Later on, General Douglas MacArthur assigned Grandpa to escort Bob Hope and his troupe on U.S.O. shows. Grandpa recalled carrying Frances Langford—a popular entertainer during the golden age of radio— piggyback along muddy roads. Langford also appeared in several films, including *Yankee Doodle Dandy* with James Cagney (she sang the song, "Over There," in that movie).

When the war finally ended in August 1945, Grandpa could have gone straight home. But Admiral Chester W. Nimitz—who signed for the United States when Japan formally surrendered aboard the U.S.S. *Missouri* in September 1945—asked Grandpa to stay on. He wanted Grandpa to serve an additional three months and help out with Operation Magic Carpet, an effort that helped repatriate around 8 million U.S. service personnel from Europe, Asia, and the Pacific.

Grandpa returned from the navy on November 22, 1945. The Bears promptly won their next two games to end the season.

college degree in, I wanted you to attend the two-year course at the Harvard University Graduate School of Business Administration. That is the best business course in the country and I want you to have a fine education in business—something I did not have...."

Some dreams take another generation.

Chapter 11

A SUPER BOWL WEDDING

I received a wonderful gift in 1982: my uncle, Jim McCaskey, called me on my 33rd birthday and gave me permission to date.

Mind you, I had been dating previously, but all those dates were illegal according to him because he had not given me permission. He taught me to say, "All that I am, all that I hope to be, is because of my Uncle Jim."

Shortly after getting the okay from Uncle Jim to date, I met Gretchen Wagle. We were introduced through mutual friends, the Bradleys and the Swiders, on Super Bowl Sunday, January 30, 1983 (Gretchen and I have reenacted the crime every year since).

I called Gretchen the next night and said, "I have a challenge for you: my parents are celebrating their 40th wedding anniversary next Saturday night. I'd like you to attend."

She said, "Gosh, that really is a challenge. I accept."

So my first date with Gretchen took place at the Notre Dame High School chapel the following Saturday. Mom and Dad renewed their wedding vows, then held a reception at the Rolling Green Country Club.

I was the master of ceremonies; Johnny Desmond sang with the help of the Dick Kress Orchestra.

All 11 of the McCaskey children were given the opportunity to address the crowd for a maximum of two minutes. (Mom told us not to talk too long because "we paid the band a lot of money.")

Here is what I said:

"We are gathered here this evening on the fourth Saturday of Ordinary Time to celebrate a most extraordinary event: George Halas is not working. You may ask why, but if you're smart you won't. The reason is obvious: his daughter Virginia and her husband Edward are still honeymooning after 40 years of marriage.

"My father is a very wise person. He has repeatedly warned his sons to watch out for young women who are interested in his sons just to become his daughters-in-law.

"My mother has often noted that my father is a very compassionate fellow. When my parents were getting married, he was very concerned about all the possible suicides.

"When my father was 17, his hair turned curly. He gave the credit to God, but he says that the girls didn't have a chance. He handled the situations by watching out for 'web-weavers'—those young women who are merely interested in getting married. When he told one of them it was over, she fainted. A month later, she was engaged to someone else.

"Then my father went to the University of Pennsylvania, and my mother went to the Drexel Institute of Technology. Both schools are located in Philadelphia. My parents-to-be noticed each other, and mutual friends set up a semi-blind date.

"George Halas sent Bert Bell and Art Rooney to the Penn campus to check out my father. He passed the test from Mr. Bell and Mr. Rooney, but not the one from Mr. Halas.

"I think my parents' marriage is a marvelous example for all of us. If you agree, please tell Mr. Halas that what we need is 40 more years."

My relationship with Gretchen was progressing nicely. She had graduated from Wheaton College, played on the tennis team, and was very intelligent. We really hit it off.

A few months later, in May, I received a pay raise with the Bears. When I thanked Dad, I said, "Now I can afford to get engaged."

"Are you thinking about that?" he asked.

"Yes, I am," I answered.

He said, "Well, Mrs. Siffermann is putting her house up for sale. Maybe you ought to take a look at it." (The Siffermanns and the McCaskeys grew up together on the same Stratford Road block in Des Plaines.)

On the Saturday of Memorial Day weekend, Gretchen and I took a close look at the Siffermann house. After the tour, Gretchen asked me, "Why are you looking for a house?"

I crossed my mouth with the back of my right hand and muttered, "In case you want to get married."

I asked her to marry me that day.

On Memorial Day, Mom asked me, "Why are you looking for a house?" (Mom and Gretchen are a lot alike, especially when it comes to being inquisitive.)

"Because Gretchen and I are talking about getting married," I said.

When Mom stopped crying with joy, she asked me, "How old is she anyway?"

"She's 30," I replied. "She only looks 18."

Mom gave us Grandma Min's engagement ring; it was a great surprise, a marvelous delight, and an outward sign that she approved of us getting married.

We did not get officially engaged until Father's Day weekend. We traveled to New Jersey that weekend because I needed to meet Gretchen's parents and ostensibly get permission.

Forget and Forgive

One evening in February 1985, I addressed the De La Salle/Joliet Catholic High School alumni banquet. One fellow in the audience was livid because the Bears had traded quarterback Bobby Layne. I pointed out that the trade took place 35 years ago and asked him to please forgive us.

On Saturday, the four of us attended a picnic at Grace Church, Gretchen's childhood church. Her father said to me, "You still have time to change your mind."

But I said, "I'm very much at peace about it."

"We are, too," he replied.

So we had permission.

Gretchen and I went to visit Grandpa on June 26—the anniversary of Grandma Min's birth. Grandpa was convalescing and looked frail for the first time in his life. He saw Gretchen with Grandma Min's ring and told us how he had purchased it more than 60 years ago.

"I bought it for $250 in a pawn shop," he said. "I wanted to make sure it was over a carat and yet I wouldn't have paid $750 for it."

Gretchen and I were married at College Church in Wheaton, Illinois, on Saturday, March 3, 1984. As I stood before Father Don Nevins and Pastor Wayne Gordon, I thought, *This is how it's going to be on the Day of Judgment. I better be a loving husband.*

Three Strikes

In 1974, I started working for the Bears, and the players went on strike. In 1982, I received a promotion, and the players went on strike. In 1987, my wife and I bought a house...and you guessed it: the players went on strike!

Gretchen and I were trying to get pregnant during the Bears' successful 1985 season—the memorable year that led to our appearance in Super Bowl XX. Unfortunately, we were unsuccessful. Doctors discovered that Gretchen had developed an ovarian cyst.

In early December, the Bears suffered their only loss of the season to the Dolphins on a Monday night in Miami 38–24. The next morning, Gretchen's cyst was removed. We would try again to get pregnant after the Super Bowl.

———

My brother Mike used a wedding analogy when he addressed family and team meetings prior to Super Bowl XX.

"Try to look at the Super Bowl as you would a wedding," he said. "There is a lot of hard work in preparing for it. There are some things that go wrong. But it is a great celebration and a lot of fun and joy for everyone."

At that point in my career with the Bears, I was the team's travel manager. My responsibility was to take care of the players and coaches in terms of meals, meetings, and practices, so my duties were of particular importance during our stay in New Orleans. However, Walter Payton—ever the practical jokester—nonetheless decided to have some fun one day at my expense. When I came into the locker room before a practice session, Payton told one of the security guards to check me out. He did and everyone involved had a good laugh.

Throughout the year, particularly the week before the Super Bowl, everyone in the Bears organization—management, coaches, and players—contributed to this history-making season, which was capped by the team's 46–10 victory over New England that made the Bears Super Bowl champions.

The night before the game, Gretchen and I had dinner with her family and another couple—Wayne and Anne Gordon—in the team hotel. We had pictures taken near the field before the game. It was the first Super Bowl I had ever attended; I only wanted to be there when the Bears played. (I'd like to attend even more Super Bowls, so let's go Bears!)

The team held a reception after the game. Gretchen and I left this bash early—at midnight! We went back to a room we shared with Wayne and Anne Gordon. The four of us engaged in a good pillow fight— my wife was my bunker—then we talked and laughed until 2:00 AM. Those Bears players who made the Pro Bowl had to leave New Orleans for Hawaii early the next morning, so they were not able to attend the downtown Chicago ticker tape parade.

Exactly nine months after the Bears' victory in Super Bowl XX, Gretchen and I were blessed with a son, Edward. He reported for duty two days early. We felt that showed good initiative; he was born Sunday, October 26, 1986, right before Kevin Butler kicked a field goal against the Detroit Lions at Soldier Field. Gretchen and I were watching the game in the delivery room at Loyola Hospital (the Bears won 13–7). If I pass away before my wife does, I hope that she finds love again, but my Super Bowl ring will go to my son Edward. All of you are witnesses!

Chapter 12
REMEMBERING MY FATHER

In the summer of 1995, Seamus Heaney was on a working vacation in Greece. When he called home to ask if there was anything new, his son replied, "Yes, you won the Nobel Prize for Literature." Here is what Seamus Heaney wrote about his father in the garden:

> *So I saw him*
> *Down on his hands and knees beside the leek rig,*
> *Touching, inspecting, separating one*
> *Stalk from the other, gently pulling up*
> *Everything not tapered, frail and leafless,*
> *Pleased to feel each little weed-root break.*

My father, Ed McCaskey, considered it a privilege to help his father in the garden. One of the things I really appreciate about my father is that he never gave up on his children. My father was not a straw boss. He worked harder than any of his children. When he cultivated the garden with a pitchfork and found one of his watches that we had buried, he could see the humor in the situation.

When I was a boy, I didn't always appreciate the change of seasons and the cycle of nature. My father said, "In the summer, we get ready for winter. In the winter, we get ready for summer."

In the summer of 1973, my father gave me the honor and the privilege of planting the garden in the north side of our yard in Des Plaines. The garden was 80 feet by six feet. It had to be roto-tilled, horse manured, roto-tilled again, and then raked smooth. I had to plant corn there and make a monumental decision: whether to put two 80-foot rows two feet apart down the length, or 39 rows two feet apart across the width. I decided to go with two 80-foot rows down the length, but it could have gone either way.

My dad (second from right, standing) on the St. Mary's basketball team. My uncle Tom is standing to his left.

Now that I am a man, I am reminded that my father never gave up on his children and that I should never give up on mine.

———

Education was very important to my father. He had graduated from St. Mary's School in Lancaster, Pennsylvania, Lancaster Catholic High School, and the University of Pennsylvania. St. Mary's School and Catholic High helped to form my father as a good Catholic, husband, brother, father, uncle, and grandfather.

His great-grandfather, John Piersol McCaskey, had been a great teacher and principal of the high school for 50 years and then mayor of the town for two terms. He was easily elected mayor because everybody who ever went to the high school carried a big coin with his picture. The inscription was, "I am one of Jack's boys."

My father came in from grade school one day for lunch. His great-grandfather said, "What did you learn in school today, young man?"

My father said, "Nothing, sir."

His great-grandfather replied, "Oh, nothing. We must never have that. Fetch the Longfellow."

So that day, before my father got lunch, he learned that

Lives of great men all remind us
We can make our lives sublime,
And, departing, leave behind us
Foot prints on the sands of time.

J.P. McCaskey believed that education is a continuing process if we are to lead rich and fulfilling lives. At Catholic High my father learned to think and to utilize the talents that God had given him. He continued to expand and enjoy all that life has to offer.

My dad was always available to lend a piece of advice to me and my siblings.

On Thursday, June 2, 1988, my father was the commencement speaker at Catholic High. He said that receiving a diploma from Lancaster Catholic High School was one of the most important things that happened in his life.

———

My father avoided death for as long as possible. On Sunday, November 9, 1969, the Bears played the Pittsburgh Steelers at Wrigley Field. The Bears won 38–7. It was the Bears' only victory that season.

My father was so excited that he had a nose bleed that wouldn't stop. He had to be taken to Holy Family Hospital for heart trouble. The doctors worked on him and he heard one doctor say, "He's gone."

My father tried to tell him "Keep trying," but he couldn't. Finally, they got him going again.

On August 9, 1986, the Bears played the Pittsburgh Steelers at Three Rivers Stadium in a preseason game. The Bears won 33–13. After the game, my father and my uncle Tom walked back to the hotel over a wooden bridge over a railroad yard. My father struggled to make it across.

A few days later, my father was sedated for heart surgery at Rush Presbyterian St. Luke's Hospital. When Dr. Najafi walked into the operating room, he said, "Let's go."

The anesthesiologist said, "Not yet, Doctor."

Dr. Najafi asked, "Why not?"

The anesthesiologist replied, "He's singing and I want to hear the end of the song."

My father beat the rap—three bypasses. After 11 months of cardiac rehab, Dr. Najafi said to my father, "Marvelous, marvelous, what you've done in cardiac rehab."

My father said, "Thank you, Doctor."

Dr. Najafi said, "Now we can do the other one."

My father asked, "What other one?"

Dr. Najafi said, "Maybe I didn't tell you. You have an aneurysm on your aorta. If that blows, you have about four minutes, but you had to be strong enough to do it."

My father said, "Thank you, Doctor. You've always been a dear friend." My father beat that one, too.

My parents often went to Mass at the Holy Family Hospital Chapel together. Several months before my father died, Father Hal got up at

Mass and mistakenly said, "Please pray for the repose of the soul of Ed McCaskey, who died yesterday."

My father got up and said, "He has risen."

My father died on Tuesday, April 8, 2003. That Saturday, his funeral took place at Maryville Academy in Des Plaines. Here is my remembrance:

> For the first six years of my parents' marriage, I was not here. I only know the legend. Three wise men from the East—Bert Bell, Bill Lennox, and Art Rooney—followed a bright star until they found my father at the University of Pennsylvania Theater. They approved of him, much to the despair of Chief Papa Bear.
>
> My mother's Indian name was Laughing Girl. My father put my mother on a donkey and they fled to Baltimore and got married. In lieu of money, they gave the donkey to the priest. More than 10 months after the wedding my brother Mike was born in Pennsylvania. He was wrapped in an army blanket and laid in an open footlocker.
>
> Across the Atlantic Ocean, Adolf Hitler had captured much of Europe. My father had heard that Hitler's ultimate plan was the capture of Ireland. So my father defeated Hitler with a sling and five smooth stones.
>
> Upon my father's return to Pennsylvania after the war, he met my brother Tim, who cried and cried at the introduction. My sister Ellen also was born there. When my mother was pregnant with me, the family moved to Illinois. Mary, Ned, Anne, George, Rich, Brian, and Joseph also were born here.
>
> I wanted to get married when I was in eighth grade because my parents had a great marriage. That was in 1963. My parents' marriage was in its 20th orbit that year.

For my 33rd birthday, my uncle Jim gave me permission to date. My first date was with Gretchen at my parents' 40th anniversary party. Now we have three sons: Ed, Tom, and James. They were named after my father and his brothers.

Thank you very much to my mother, my brothers and sisters, the Bears' trainers, my father's doctors and nurses, and all of you for taking great care of my father.

My father kept after me to get a corneal transplant. This past Monday I did. I don't know who the donor was, but my father was the inspiration.

It's wonderful that all of us are here. Each of us was my father's favorite.

My mom and dad share a happy moment.

Chapter 13
WORDS OF WISDOM

O n January 22, 1972, my grandfather spoke in Washington, D.C. Here is part of the speech my father wrote for him:

For me, it is impossible to visit our nation's capital without feeling a surge of pride, for this is the heart of America, the greatest nation on earth—your country, my country, our country, the United States of America....

Football has been my life. I drifted into it a long time ago with no preparation except four years under Zuppke at Illinois and an abiding itch. Fifty years ago I fell in love with the kickoff sound of a foot striking leather and have been stuck with it ever since....

How could I dream those short 50 years ago that 65 million people would see the Dallas Cowboys play the Miami Dolphins in Super Bowl VI? How could I dream that in 1972 the Gallup Poll would reveal football as America's No. 1 spectator sport?

I could not and I did not.... The miracle to me is not that football has grown to be the No. 1 spectator sport, but rather the important place that football has in the lives of millions of Americans. Today, with so much of the earth destroyed, damaged, or at least endangered, with heartache and turmoil surrounding us, a man's courage can easily fail him. Surrounded as we are by a sea of bad news, how does one find the strength to continue? I have long been fascinated by the adventures of Jacques Cousteau, who tells us that the sea is dying. He has been down there, so he must know. Many say our cities are dying, and if the cities die, so will civilization as we know it. But we must never despair, for despair is no good for any of us...and so I would suggest to you that professional football has become a beacon of light for the millions of Americans who thrill to its excitement.

Recently Commissioner [Pete] Rozelle authorized Louis Harris and Associates to undertake a survey of a cross section of sports fans in the country. When asked "What does pro football do for you?" the fans surveyed answered in a manner which I found fascinating. For example: "entertainment and enjoyment"..."relaxation and recreation"..."thrilling and exciting"..."draws the family together when we watch it"..."gives us something to talk to friends about"... "an outlet for letting off steam"..."something to look forward to on the weekend"..."makes me feel young!" That's my favorite, "makes me feel young!" With this survey in mind I would make bold to suggest to those few members of the Congress who are less than enthusiastic about football that they think seriously before taking any action which would hamper the continued growth of professional football.

I say this without interest...I have reached the stage in life where, thanks to football and good luck, I have everything I need. In fact, I only buy one shirt at a time and I avoid magazines because I don't want to start any continued stories.

My concern is for the great game of football and for the salubrious effect that it has on millions of fans in America. My appeal is to any and all of you who can do so, to do all that you can to enhance the climate for football. We don't need detractors...we do need football in America.

Parenting Athletes

For several years, I didn't want to coach my sons on their sports teams because I figured I coach them a lot at home. It's still a game of courtesy and grammar; I wanted them to get a different perspective. Besides, every time they did something right in a game, I'd want to call timeout and shellac the ball.

However, when my sons were in the seventh and eighth grades, I took it upon myself to be one of their football coaches. I was, after all, an expert for a long time. Before most games, I said to my sons, "Good luck. Do your best because God doesn't grade on a curve. If you do your best, you're a winner regardless of the score."

When my son Ed was in eighth grade, his team finished second. When my son Tom was in eighth grade, his team captured first place. When my son James was in eighth grade, the team again took first place.

When I wasn't coaching, my goal as a parent was to show interest without meddling. In my mind, any playing time they received was a great opportunity for them. I would take notes at my sons' games. My approach to chronicling their efforts was, "You were given this much playing time and this is what you did with it." I provided accountability and encouragement. I showed my notes to my sons, but I never bothered their coaches. Taking notes at the games helped keep me quiet; then I wasn't tempted to coach or officiate from the stands (when my sons played, of course, I thought their coaches were great).

Once I had a great friend who paused for too short a time on this earth, in this country, in this city. Once he said: "Football symbolizes the attributes of America: stamina, courage, teamwork, self-denial, sportsmanship, selflessness, and respect for authority. The struggle America faces today is a struggle for the hearts and souls and minds of men. Unlike football where there are millions of spectators and only a few players, the struggle of life is a game in which there are no spectators, but where everyone is a player."

My friend's name was Vince Lombardi. Thank you.

On October 3, 1977, Jim Finks asked my father to address the Bears' wives' luncheon. Here is what he said:

Thank you very much, Jim, for introducing me to this lovely group. When I say lovely, I mean just that. Memory does not help me to recall so many beautiful women gathered in one single space. We are very proud of our Chicago Bears players and now that I have met all of you, we are prouder than ever. I am confident that each of you does your very best to encourage your special man to do well at practice and on game day. However, there is another responsibility which I would like to ask you to consider, and because you enjoy the full flush of beauty and of youth, it may have escaped your attention.

These Chicago Bear players are truly special men. Consider the fact that each year our colleges and universities graduate approximately 5,000 football players. Of the 5,000 who graduated, less than 500 are drafted into the NFL. Of the number that are drafted, the best four or five find a place on the rosters of their respective clubs. Truly, these are gifted athletes. Theirs is a glorious opportunity. They have a chance to play a game that they love, receive the adulation of their fans, and in the process make a great deal of money, and that is the area which I would like to bring to your attention today.

For men their age, professional football players today make a tremendous amount of money. I would urge each of you to counsel with your husband and encourage him to save and invest soundly every penny that you can spare. Football is merely a stepping-stone to life's work. All too soon, your husband's playing days will be finished, and you will be faced with the reality of the business world which pays far less than football. Therefore, I urge you to help your husbands prepare for the day when they must retire. If your husband does not have his degree, urge him to obtain it in the off-season. If he leans toward graduate school, help him to go on. If he has completed his schooling, make certain that he utilizes the off-season to gain business experience and start preparing for retirement.

Your football paychecks will help you to obtain a tremendous head start on life, and if ever I can be of assistance to any one of you and your husband in counseling for the future, it will be a pleasure to help you. Most of all, I hope you will be happy with the Chicago Bears and proud to be members of our family. I am delighted that you are here, and I ask only that in your prayers, remember the Bears.

Several former Chicago Bears—fullback Bob Christian, defensive end Richard Dent, and place-kicker Bob Thomas—spoke at the Notre Dame High School Sports Night on February 17, 1994. Ray Gorzynski (class of 1960) served as master of ceremonies. He and Joe Gurdak, John Ranos ('66), Bob Byrne ('67), and George Skinner comprised the Sports Night committee.

Christian said, "Early in my life, I made a commitment to the Lord and to serve Him in everything I do. Proverbs 21:31 says, 'The horse is equipped for the day of battle, but victory is the Lord's.' I had faith that God had me in his hands. I did my best to prepare. He took care of the outcome.

"God taught me a great lesson about who I am. We should be thankful for the opportunities that we have. Just having the opportunity is such a blessing. Coming out of college, the team that I really wanted to play for was the Bears.

"God showed me a verse, Psalm 37:4: 'Take delight in the Lord, and He will grant you your heart's requests.' All you kids who are shooting for a goal, whatever you set your mind for, keep working for it and keep your faith in God. Seek after him. He'll open doors for you and you'll be able to walk through them."

Dent then said, "It's nice to see some of you young fellows who are trying to find your goals and dreams in life. I'm going to tell you about mine and what I stand for and how I got to where I am today. I started playing football in 10th grade. I think that role models start within the family. You have to have someone you can look up to.

"I am very fortunate. Regardless of what round you get drafted in, you have to come in and go to work. Life doesn't owe you anything. It's what you make of life. Everyone wants to be someone that other people respect and like. You have to take care of your body. You have to be dedicated to what you want to do. If you work hard and have faith in God, everything will fall down in its place.

"When you talk about me and what I stand for, I am dedicated. I am educated. I study film and read about my opponents. After football, education helps for my second phase of life.

"You have to be thankful, to be proud of who you are. You have to be thankful for everything. You should always pray and always be thankful you have something special, deep down inside of yourself. Someday, some of you may come back here to talk about your success."

Richard's Make a Dent Foundation, founded in the 1990s, is focused on improving the lives of children.

Bob Thomas then said, "Because I played 10 years for the Bears and now that I'm a judge...I have a pulpit, but I don't have a monopoly on disappointments. When we do, we look at them in terms of fairness and justice. As an aside, I'd like to say, I thank our Lord that he thinks in terms of mercy. Otherwise none of us would be in heaven someday. My God was good to me."

On February 14, 1995, the fourth annual sports night took place in the cafeteria of Notre Dame High School. Then–Chicago Bears director of player personnel Rod Graves, assistant head coach/offensive line coach Tony Wise, and defensive lineman Alonzo Spellman were the speakers. Graves talked about faith, Wise talked about teamwork, and Spellman talked about family and education.

Graves said, "My wife grew up in a family where alcoholism was prevalent. When we were married, she brought to the family quite a bit of baggage. The thing that we were not able to overcome was the communication problem. There was no real intimacy in regard to conversation, to feeling that we were together. I was almost ready to give up on marriage.

"Some of us reach points in our lives where circumstances are so great, where we think we don't have enough power to really overcome those circumstances. We would really just fold up and quit.

"At this particular juncture, I decided to give up on doing things myself and to put it all in the hands of God. I decided to concentrate heavily on myself and leave the rest to God. At that point, I began to pray quite a bit, not only for my wife, but for me and to stop trying to rectify our problems with my own power.

"My marriage is one of the most beautiful and healthiest marriages there is. It's solely because I took a new perspective on dealing with the problems and dealing with myself and the way I viewed my approach to people and the way I viewed my approach to my wife."

Wise said, "Teamwork is one of the most important things that you must have to be a successful team. I don't want to be known as a star on a rotten team. I'd rather be a pretty good player on a team and be recognized at the end of the year as a Super Bowl champ or a district champ or a state champ. We preach teamwork to our guys all the time.

"Teamwork requires sacrifice. You've got to sacrifice your own performance so that the team can be successful. I coach the offensive line, which is really the height of teamwork. We've got five guys in there who have to sacrifice themselves in order for the rest of the team to do well.

"We've got guys who work and sacrifice. How much do you respect the guy next to you? How much does he respect you? When he makes a mistake, are you willing to let that slide and say, 'I know he's working as hard as he can'? I know that next play, he's going to come out and try as hard as he can to win....

"The thing you guys have got to remember when you watch the Bears play is that it's not one guy doing one thing. It's a team game. It will always be a team game. The more you work together with your teammates, the more you encourage your teammates, the more success each and every one of you will have."

Spellman said, "There are three things that I live by and encourage others to live by. The first is the Lord is extremely important in my life. The second is my family. The third is my job and where I work. For you, that should be education. You should work hard in school and listen to your parents telling you to pull your grades up, to study after school, to work very hard and ask questions in the classroom.

"The Lord is very important in my life because he gives me the ability to go out and be myself. He opens doors for me that without my faith in the Lord would otherwise be closed. If you have faith, you switch all your sights to the Lord. You say, I'm going to work very hard at school. I'm going to do my homework and listen to my mother.

"The way all that works and happens for you is by faith. If you have faith, you won't look at your math test after studying three or four night and get nervous and think that you can't do it. Those feelings won't be there if the Lord is in your life.

"Another extremely important part of my life is my family. I'm from the inner city. My family has always been behind me. Now that I'm in the National Football League, I probably need them most. My mother raised six children in a two-bedroom apartment. The main thing she always told me was to never quit.

"In closing, understand that it is very important that you take control of your life. You should straighten up your room. You should come home after school and do your homework. You should do responsible things in the house. You will be building a strong foundation for you to have a better life."

———

The fifth annual Sports Night took place in the cafeteria of Notre Dame High School in February 1996. The speakers were Leslie Frazier—cornerback for the Super Bowl XX champion Bears and currently the defensive coordinator for the Minnesota Vikings—Bears offensive coordinator Ron Turner, and *Pro Football Weekly* publisher and Chicago sports-radio commentator Hub Arkush.

During his talk, Frazier—who was born in Columbus, Mississippi—mentioned that his grandmother raised him. As a young student-athlete, he dreamed of becoming a professional football player, and he tried to emulate Gale Sayers.

Frazier pointed out that his upbringing at home helped him to become a success. He said that his son once asked him, "Dad, if I don't become a professional football player, would you be mad at me?" Frazier replied, "Your mom and I want you to love God with all your heart no matter what you decide to do with the rest of your life."

Growing up, Frazier said he avoided drugs and alcohol. He encouraged parents in the crowd to be positive role models for their children and to help them deal with peer pressures.

Meanwhile, Turner talked about the importance of having a close-knit family. The youngest of five children, Turner was just 10 months old when his father deserted the family. Later, his mother was diagnosed with multiple sclerosis. The family grew up in a housing project in northern California and was raised on welfare until his mother remarried.

Turner said his mother, who passed away in 1989, never complained about anything. She talked about God, religion, faith, believing in yourself, believing in each other, and supporting each other. He said she emphasized the positive, never the negative. She stressed to her family that they had to treat people the way they wanted to be treated. She taught them right from wrong and to make the right choice.

Today, Turner, his brothers, and his sisters are very close. They talk with each other and write each other quite often. The support is always there for one another.

Turner and his wife Wendy have four children; they are a very strong family. Because of what he went through during his childhood, Turner makes sure he is there for Wendy and the kids.

When Arkush took the podium, he talked about his oldest son, who was a high school senior, a football player, and a wrestler. He just missed going downstate in wrestling by one point, and was very upset that he didn't go to the state tournament.

Arkush put his arm around his son and asked him, "How do you feel? What's the problem?" He replied, "It's over. I may never wrestle again." But Arkush also pointed out that his son "began to grasp how fleeting this all is. How you better grab and enjoy it because you're going to blink and it's going to be gone."

The family of the wrestler that defeated Arkush's son "were cheering; they were having a great time. They thought this was the greatest thing they had ever seen." Arkush went over to the other wrestler's father and shook his hand. "It was a great moment for them," Arkush said.

"What you get from the competition is the competition itself," Arkush said. "What you get from the ability is the lesson to be learned in victory and the lesson to be learned in defeat…

"That end is your family and the people around you and the joy you give them and the joy you take from them and what you've learned together to be better people to share with everyone else in your community.

"That said, if the Bears get another Super Bowl, we'll all have a better community next year."

In 1998, the Chicago Bears were approached with the concept of visiting Chicago Public Schools. The idea was for Bears personnel to visit schools on Tuesdays and talk about the importance of education. The Bears would help students develop character, commit to excellence, and learn how to set and achieve goals.

This idea was particularly appealing to me because of my family's history. My great-great-grandfather, John Piersol McCaskey, was a teacher and a principal for more than 50 years in Lancaster, Pennsylvania. In 1867, he wrote the song *Jolly Old Saint Nicholas*. After he died, the school was named after him (McCaskey High School). Here are some quotes from J.P.'s writings:

> *To assume that ability to spell, naming the letters of a word in their appointed order; to read, calling words at sight, often with little apprehension of the thought; to cipher, with fair degree of accuracy in mechanical results—these things are "education!" and here to pause, is to be content with a very low standard of attainment. It is to live in the sub-cellar of a palace, when you might command, if you so desired, a broad outlook from spacious windows higher up in the free air of heaven, under the stars.*
>
> *Education runs out on so many lines! It has to do with nature and art and life and the things of Time and the dream of Eternity.*

It takes in acquaintance with books, but no less the butterfly and the bird, the grass and the flower, the leaf and the habit of the tree, the billowy wheat, the rustling corn, the wind and cloud, air and earth, and sea and sky, with their myriad wonders of animate and inanimate creation; music, with its melody and harmony; gratitude to our fellows for the many good things in which we should hold ourselves their debtors, and to God, "In whom we live and move and have our being."

ACKNOWLEDGMENTS

Over the years, many writers and authors have chronicled the history of my family and the Chicago Bears. Among the many books I consulted during the writing of this book: *Bulldogs on Sunday* by the Pro Football Research Association; *The Chicago Bears*, by Howard Roberts; *That's How the Ball Bounces....*, by George Halas; *Pro Football's Rag Days*, by Bob Curran; *The First 50 Years: The Story of the National Football League; The NFL's Official Encyclopedia of Professional Football; The Scrapbook History of Pro Football;* and *The Sports Encyclopedia: Pro Football*, by David Neft, Roland Johnson, Richard Cohen, and Jordan Deutsch; *More Than a Game*, by John Wiebusch; *200 Years of Sport in America*, by Wells Twombly; *Football (A Love Story)*, by Edward McCaskey; *Victory After the Game: The Harlon Hill Story*, by Ronnie Thomas; *Pro Football At Its Best*, by Jack Fleischer; *Grif*, by Woodson Jack Griffin; *Halas by Halas: The Autobiography of George Halas*, by George Halas with Gwen Morgan and Arthur Veysey; *The Chicago Bears: An Illustrated History; The Fireside Book of Pro Football; Bears in Their Own Words; The Bears: A 75-Year Celebration;* and *What a Game They Played*, by Richard Whittingham; *Champions of American Sport*, written and edited by Marc Pachter with Amy Henderson, Jeannette Hussey, and Margaret C.S. Christman; *Letters to Baby*, by Chaz Corzine; *The Official*

NFL Encyclopedia of Pro Football; *To Absent Friends* and *The Red Smith Reader*, by Red Smith; *Their Deeds and Dogged Faith*, by Mike Rathet and Don R. Smith; *The New Thinking Man's Guide to Pro Football*, by Paul Zimmerman; *NFL Top 40: The Greatest Pro Football Games of All Time*, by Shelby Strother; *The Bob Verdi Collection*, by Bob Verdi; *Humility of Greatness*, by Ken Kavanaugh Jr.; *Tom Landry: An Autobiography*, by Tom Landry; *War Stories from the Field*, by Joseph Hession and Kevin Lynch; and *Total Football: The Official Encyclopedia of the National Football League*, edited by Bob Carroll, Michael Gershman, David Neft, and John Thorn.

Several periodicals, including newspapers operated by the NorthWest News Group and the Pioneer Press, were invaluable in checking assorted facts. I was also fortunate enough to speak to dozens of men and women, as well as read letters they wrote to one another. They include Neill Armstrong, J.R. Boone, Jim Canady, Rick Casares, Ed Cifers, Harper Davis, Elaine Dooley, Kayo Dottley, Thelma Farris, Tom Farris, Aldo Forte, Bill George, Helen Geyer, Abe Gibron, Jack Griffin, Dave Hale, Dallas Himm, Bob Hope, Mike Hull, Ted Karras, Ken Kavanaugh Jr., Lee Kunz, Virgil Livers, Bob MacLeod, Chuck Mather, George McAfee, Bill McColl, Ookie Miller, Don Mullins, Bill Osmanski, Mac Percival, Bob Pifferini, Paul Podmajersky, Libby Preston, Jim Purnell, Robert Ray, Tom Roggeman, Brad Rowland, Steve Sabol, Gene Schroeder, Bob Snyder, Ed Sprinkle, Mary Jo Thompson, Clyde Turner, Bill Wade, Byron White, and Chris Willis.

Appendix A

George Halas'
Induction to the
Pro Football Hall of Fame

On Saturday, September 7, 1963, my grandfather was inducted into the Pro Football Hall of Fame. Here is what he said:

Thank you, Governor Lawrence, ladies and gentlemen. A few weeks ago a few of our grandchildren visited the Bears' training camp and I was talking to them about the trip to Canton to participate in the dedication of Pro Football's Hall of Fame. Somehow the conversation got around to an earlier trip that I made to Canton some 43 years ago when we met in Ralph Hay's automobile showroom and founded the National Football League. I told them some of the informal aspects of that meeting and among them being that there was a lack of chairs and also that we had to sit on the running board of the car. That prompted my nine-year-old grandson to say, "What is a running board, Grandpa?" I [was about to answer] when my 14-year-old grandson said, "Running boards are those things that you see on those funny, old cars in that television series known as *The Untouchables*." That little incident demonstrated to me how things can change or disappear until a chance remark or a question—a child's question—stirs your memory.

On my trip down here, my memory was stirred back quite a few years when I think of the wonderful men who did so much to develop football in this area and through the country. Such fellas like the Nesser brothers, Ralph Hay, Frank McNeil, Leo Lyons, Joe Carr of the Columbus Panhandles, who was president of the National Football League from 1921 to 1939, some 18 years, and you may be sure that some of those years were pretty tough. They were the pioneers and this is the land where football sat down its roots, and here is the Hall of Fame where its history and traditions will be preserved and remembered.

To all of you who have contributed so much to the realization of this Hall of Fame—you people of Canton, Mr. Umstattd [William E. Umstattd of the Timken Company who spearheaded efforts to get the Hall of Fame in Canton], and all the rest of you—let me say for all the Chicago Bears right from the original Staleys in 1920 down to the 1963, just two heartfelt words: thank you!

Appendix B

GALE SAYERS
RECEIVES THE GEORGE HALAS
AWARD FOR COURAGE

In 1969, Gale Sayers led the NFL in rushing with 1,032 yards on 236 carries. After the season, he received the George Halas Award for Courage:

Of all the honors I have been fortunate enough to receive, I must say in all honesty that tonight's holds the greatest meaning for me. I am most humble when I read the engraved words that describe the reason for it—the George S. Halas Award for Courage.

It is appropriate that Mr. Halas' name should be identified with this award because the record shows that he is and has always been a man of courage. Needless to say, my five years' association with Mr. Halas increased my admiration for him—and I am proud and grateful to accept an award sponsored by a man for whom I feel great affection.

But to return to my part in all of this tonight, something very personal is represented in this award.

There were skeptics—and there probably still are some—who wrote or said what they must have believed firmly—that Gale Sayers would never bring back the full 100 percent of his ability to football, especially a certain expert who spent a lot of time at our training camp. At the occasional sessions when I'd leave off the pads and just go around in shorts and a T-shirt, he would come up to me, bend over, put his hands on his knees, and stare at my knee as he'd ask the question that was beginning to irritate me—"Gale, do you think you'll ever cut or move the way you used to do?"

He didn't know that inside of me there was a fierce determination to prove my worth, to prove my mettle. I never set my heart or sharpened my physique so intensely as I did for the 1969 season. The day after my operation I began my exercises and I never stopped them until they were superseded by the routine of training camp in July. I was determined to come back and play as well as ever, and the fact that I did is the most satisfying experience in my life.

It is something special to do a job that few people say can't be done. Maybe that's how courage is spelled out—at least in my case. Although there were detractors, there were also a few people who never stopped believing in me and encouraging me to keep driving. I'd like to acknowledge their support, here and now—especially our team physician, Dr. Ted Fox, Coach Halas and Buddy Young, to commissioner Pete Rozelle, and my teammate, roommate, and friend, Brian Piccolo.

Brian Piccolo, who in a humorous, kindly, and sometimes unkindly way, urged me day after day to fight my way back. Brian Piccolo, who has the sheer, solid, raw courage, which entitles him to win over a sickness that makes my knee injury seem unimportant.

In the middle of last season, Brian was struck down by the deadliest, most shocking enemy any of us can ever face—cancer. Compare his courage with that which I am supposed to possess, as symbolized by this award. There was never any doubt in my mind that I'd run again, knee injury or no. But think of Brian and his courage and fortitude shown in the months since last November: in and out of hospitals, hoping to play football again, but not too sure at any time what the score was or might be. But Brian Piccolo has never given up because he has the heart of a giant and that rare form of courage that allows him to kid himself and his opponent—cancer. He has the mental attitude that makes me proud to have a friend who spells out the word *courage* 24 hours a day, every day of his life.

You flatter me by giving me this award, but I tell you here and now that I accept it for Brian Piccolo. Brian Piccolo is the man of courage who should receive the George S. Halas Award. I accept it tonight and I'll present it to Brian tomorrow. I love Brian Piccolo and I'd like all of you to love him, too.

Tonight when you hit your knees, please ask God to love him— thank you!

Appendix C

JOY PICCOLO

SPEAKS IN INDIANAPOLIS

In January 1972, Brian Piccolo's widow, Joy, made a speech in Indianapolis:

Since the viewing of *Brian's Song* on ABC Television several months ago, I have been inundated with requests to appear and to speak. Most of the requests have been from very worthwhile groups determined to do something to defeat cancer....

Because of my responsibility to my three daughters, Lori, Traci, and Kristi, I feel it is necessary to decline most of these requests...in fact, I originally declined to appear here today. However, when I considered the great sacrifices you have made and the hopeful and exciting work you are doing, I did decide to come....

I am very glad I did, for you have been very kind and gracious to me. All of America has been kind to me and I am most grateful.... Brian's appeal to people from all walks of life is reflected in the continuing growth of the Brian Piccolo Cancer Research Fund at Memorial Hospital in New York City. There, Dr. Beattie and his staff are joining with you in a mighty effort to win over cancer...if we all continue to try we must win and win we will...

Tonight when I return home the girls will run to me and ask, "Mommy, where were you today and what did you do?" When I tell them I was with you and of the work you are doing, I'll also ask them to pray for you....

My daughters inherited all of their father's best features and they are truly beautiful.... So you rest assured that tonight my little beauties, Lori, Traci, and Kristi, will ask God to bless you all.... Surely he won't deny the request of three little angels who allowed their mother to be here with you today. Thank you!

The film Brian's Song *advertised on the marquee at the Michael Todd Theater in Chicago.*

Appendix D

BILL GEORGE'S
INDUCTION TO THE
PRO FOOTBALL HALL OF FAME

My father, Ed McCaskey, presented Bill George for induction into the
Pro Football Hall of Fame on July 27, 1974:

What are the qualities that make men great? I'm not sure that I know, but in professional football they are thought to be ability, dedication, desire, and courage.

In 1952 Bill George came from Wake Forest to the Chicago Bears, bringing with him those four qualities in abundance. He was installed immediately as the Bears' middle as all teams were playing a five-man defensive front. Bill continued at middle guard until 1954 when in a Bear–Eagle game he dropped back and intercepted the first of 18 passes during his illustrious career.

Due to Bill's innovative maneuver, a new position was born—middle linebacker—and both offense and defense changed throughout the National Football League.

Then in the early '60s, the 49ers terrorized all opposition with their vaunted shotgun attack. In the two games preceding the Bears, the 49ers had rolled up over 1,000 yards with the shotgun. Under the tutelage of a true football genius, Clark Shaughnessy, Bill George moved into his old middle guard position, barreled past the 49er center, and dumped the quarterback time after time. That day in Wrigley Field, the 49ers gained only 132 yards—and as a total offensive weapon, the shotgun was consigned to the scrap pile.

For 14 years Bill George played in the NFL and in eight of those years, he was an All-Pro selection.

Bill George was a leader—and how he led the Bear defense! Coach Halas once said of him that having Bill on the field was like having a coach in the lineup.

Great athletes know glory—at times adversity is their lot. In 1962, Bill suffered a severe neck injury in an auto accident. Despite terrible pain, he played the entire season and in 1963, he led the Bears to the world championship. In 1964, he injured his knee and missed six games,

Bill George played 14 years for the Chicago Bears.

and in 1965, he played in only two games. Nineteen sixty-six was the last year of his football career when he played 14 games for the Los Angeles Rams.

Far more important than his football skills are his qualities of humility and generosity. Equally important as his great football career is his ability to inspire the young people with whom he has contact. He is tireless in his efforts on behalf of youngsters.

No matter how wet, cold, or hungry my own children were, they never left Wrigley Field until they had at least a glimpse of Bill talking to the crowd of youngsters that never failed to surround him after Bear home games.

Of all the athletes I have known, I think Bill George knows best how to handle the fragile burden of the adulation of the very young.

My personal debt to Bill George is boundless, for he gave me a very treasured gift.

In March of 1966, he asked me to see him privately and told me that he would not be with the Bears that year. He asked me to get to know and to keep an eye on a young man who had just finished his rookie season with the Bears. He described him as a very special person. How special he was!

Little did I dream that night that only one year later I would be working for the Bears as liaison man among the owners, the coaches, and the players. By then I had come to know Bill's special person very well.

He returned my small favors by making certain that I was accepted by the Bear veterans. He became my friend, then my son. His name was Brian Piccolo.

How proud Bill's mother must be today. He has been a credit to his sister, his brothers, his daughter, and his sons, Leo and Biff—to the Chicago Bears family and to all who comprise this great sport of football.

It is a privilege to present him for induction into the Pro Football Hall of Fame.

Appendix E

GEORGE CONNOR'S
INDUCTION TO THE
PRO FOOTBALL HALL OF FAME

*On Saturday, August 2, 1975, my grandfather presented George Connor
for induction into the Pro Football of Fame:*

This day is something special for four exceptional big-league football
players who have had many memorable days in the past, but none quite
as special or as memorable as today when these four will be the 1975
inductees into the Professional Football Hall of Fame.

My presence on this dais makes today something special for me
personally, too. It is my privilege to do the formal honors of presentation
of one of the four National Football League greats, George Connor, who
brings the Chicago Bears' membership in the Hall up to 15…or exactly
the NFL player limit way back in the misty 1920s.

As one of 17 charter members of the Hall—and the first of the Bears
to be so honored—I still remember my own induction day of September
7, 1963, when this great facility was dedicated.

I experienced emotion unlike anything in my athletic career, a thrill
that takes precedence over any I have experienced before or since.

So, I can understand and share with these all-time pro greats the overwhelming sense of ecstasy that is theirs on *this* day—*their* day—the ultimate recognition of their greatness in the sport that they chose as a career.

I am proud of George Connor, and grateful as well for his competitive contributions to the Bears. To me—and maybe to others, too—he seems to be physically as massive and threatening today as he was in his NFL seasons.

He towered 6'3" and hasn't shrunk with the years. He came in at 240 pounds playing weight, and I'll leave it up to him whether he has added any poundage. He had and he still has a chest measurement of 53 inches expanded from 48 inches normal.

The sight of this solid, muscular athlete in action once inspired the late sportswriter Grantland Rice to observe, "Connor is the closest thing to a Greek god since Apollo."

Well, I still have some notes from the time that appeared in print sent to me by more than a few of George's Irish-American friends from the South Side of Chicago.

They topped Grantland Rice by pointing out that history showed the Connors were kings of Ireland—such strong leaders as Connor Mor, who reigned in the early centuries...or Connor MacNess, one of his successors...not to mention the fabulous Connor of the Hundred Battles who lost only 10—and virtually all of those defeats were questionable decisions.

So George Connor came from stock that was real flesh and blood, not just legendary. He was one of the last of football's ironmen—the 60-minute players who went all the way on offense and defense. Five times, he was chosen All-NFL, and three of those times, he had the very rare distinction of being picked on both offense and defense—tackle on offense plus linebacker on defense two seasons and defensive tackle one season.

It would be difficult for me to go on record as saying where he excelled—I would rather have had three like him, but I feel fortunate to have *one* Connor for eight seasons.

He is Chicago born-and-bred—but he had a lot of growing to do from a tiny acorn to a mighty oak. His was a premature birth and he weighed only three pounds.

As a freshman at De La Salle High School in Chicago, he weighed 135 and stood 5'4", but three years later, he was 6'2", 215.

His collegiate days were divided—first at Holy Cross, during World War II, when he was an All-American in 1943 as a freshman; and then Notre Dame, where he was twice All-American.

We of the Bears were fortunate that George insisted he would play his pro football only in Chicago, his hometown, even though he had been drafted No. 1 by the Boston Yanks. We traded Mike Jarmoluk, a two-year NFL veteran tackle from Temple, for the negotiation rights to George, and he signed with us.

His career was shortened by at least five seasons by a knee injury in the preseason of 1954. He managed part-time service that season but in 1955, he came back with his best NFL season. Then, during training camp of 1956, he came up to me one day and said, "Coach, I can't do the job any more...it's my knee again and I don't want to be a hanger-on."

So many games and individual plays or sequence of plays come to mind when I think of George Connor that I just can't isolate any as his greatest performance.

He just simply was great all the way—born to heroics and completely at ease and efficient in the role.

George Connor, I bid you welcome to Pro Football's Hall of Fame where you deservedly join some other Bears as well as other immortals from other teams.

Congratulations!

Appendix F

GALE SAYERS'
INDUCTION TO THE
PRO FOOTBALL HALL OF FAME

My grandfather presented Gale Sayers for induction into the Pro Football Hall of Fame on Saturday, July 30, 1977:

It is indeed a thrill for me to be here again at the Pro Football Hall of Fame. The great city of Canton with its great people have always made me feel so at home. My memories of Canton go all the way back to 1920. Then, I sat on a running board in Ralph Hay's auto agency when we formed what is now the NFL. And I can remember hoping that they were only kidding when they said that franchises would cost $100. Where in the world would I have gotten $100? But I have over a hundred now thanks to all the men who strove through the years to make the NFL the great institution it is today. Many of those men have been enshrined in our Hall of Fame, and today another group of great football players will take their places with the immortals who have made football a way of life in America.

Today, Frank Gifford, Forrest Gregg, Bart Starr, and Bill Willis will take their rightful places as members of the Hall of Fame. Each of these men have, from time to time, done their very best to break my heart, and each of them has done that job very well. Each of them has contributed to sleepless nights for me for each of them has managed to help defeat my beloved Bears. So I'll say no more about them except to congratulate them on being honored here today. Instead I'll tell you about their fellow enshrinee who stole my heart: Gale Sayers. Gale Sayers! Magic in motion!

The first time I saw Gale Sayers, it was on film. After one of my assistants ran that film, I was puzzled. I wasn't certain of what I had seen, so I asked that the film be run again and again! And again! I knew that it wasn't Red Grange! I knew that it wasn't George McAfee! But I knew that what I was watching was very, very special, and I was determined that Gale Sayers would become a Chicago Bear.

It wasn't easy to obtain his services because Lamar Hunt also wanted Gale badly; however, Buddy Young helped us to convince Gale to sign with the Bears, and I shall always be grateful to Buddy.

When I met Gale I was surprised by his modesty and his unassuming manner. In practice he was a 100 percenter. On run plays he always ran to the goal line and he was always razor-sharp physically. His teammates respected and admired him and never begrudged him the publicity he received. Gale recognized that all of his inherent skills would mean little without the help of his blockers, and he expressed gratitude to his teammates.

Gale's opponents respected him as well. I'll never forget that on the afternoon of his first injury, a knee injury which resulted from a clean tackle by Kermit Alexander of the 49ers, that after the game Kermit came to the Bear dressing room to assure Gale that he was sorry that happened.

Gale Sayers had many great games as a Chicago Bear. In his rookie year he scored 22 touchdowns, and one rainy afternoon on a muddy field he scored six touchdowns against San Francisco. So many great games! One such game was at Green Bay when we won 13–10 and Gale ran for 205 yards and Vince Lombardi's accolade that it was the finest performance he ever saw.

Once in Minnesota, the Vikings had gone ahead 37–31, and on the kickoff following their touchdown Gale ran 96 yards and we went ahead 38–37. The Vikings started another march and [Dick] Butkus intercepted and Gale rammed into the end zone and we won 45–37. So many great games!

But Gale's greatest performance was not on the football field. After his serious injury in 1968, Gale came back in 1969 to lead the NFL in rushing with over 1,000 yards. For this remarkable feat he received the award as the most courageous player at the New York Football Writers Dinner. When he received the trophy, Gale said, "Tonight, this trophy is mine—tomorrow it will be Brian's." The next day he gave the trophy to Brian Piccolo, his roommate and friend—a man of courage.

Gale Sayers is the youngest man ever inducted into the Pro Football Hall of Fame.

Earlier I told you that I sat on that running board in 1920. I played for the Bears for 10 years. I coached for 40 years and I have owned the Chicago Bears for 57 years, so I feel that I speak with authority today. In 57 years I have seen them all. Today I tell you that if you would see perfection at running back you had best get a film of Gale Sayers. He was poetry in motion and we shall never see his like again.

Gale Sayers, at age 34, is the athletics director at Southern Illinois University. Gale Sayers, at age 34, is the youngest man to ever be inducted into the Hall of Fame. Gale—you know that I never tried to teach you how to run. The secret something that you possessed God gave you and no mortal could improve it, so I never tried to do so.

With a father's love and all the affection one man is allowed to have for another, I proudly present for induction into the Hall of Fame Gale Sayers of the Chicago Bears.

Appendix G

RESOLUTION FOR UNCLE MUGS

My father wrote a resolution for the Bears' board of directors after Mugs Halas died:

It is fitting and proper that the members of the board of directors of the Chicago Bears Football Club avail themselves of the opportunity at this time to acknowledge their heartfelt sorrow due to the death of the president, George Halas Jr. It is equally fitting and proper that the board acknowledge the countless contributions of Mugs to the success and well-being of the Chicago Bears Football Club.

George "Mugs" Halas was born on September 4, 1925. Commencing from the time that he was a toddler he was completely devoted to his father, which was tantamount to being completely devoted to the Chicago Bears, for they are one and the same. After a long and fruitful apprenticeship, Mugs became president of the Bears in 1963 and retained that post for 17 years until his death on December 16, 1979.

Mugs Halas served the Bears in remarkable fashion. During his stewardship there were the usual highs and lows that mark this great sport, but whatever the fortunes on the playing field the business aspects of the Bears remained sound under Mugs' leadership. As a result of Mugs' knowledge of football and his outstanding ability to make sound business judgments, the Bears are in excellent financial and competitive positions today.

Mugs' greatest strengths lay in his relations with his fellow owners and peers. His reputation for integrity and honesty enhanced his business acumen in his handling of league affairs. His was long the voice of reason in the difficult negotiations with the players' union.

Mugs served as a member of the Management Council which worked so hard to gain agreement with the union. Because of his innate sense of fairness and his lifelong devotion to his father's house, Mugs was able to effect the settlement of many thorny issues.

In league matters, it was an accepted fact that when the owners reached an impasse, sooner or later his peers would turn to Mugs for a solution. His integrity, his honesty, and his decency far outweighed his lack of tact. He was respected, and in many cases loved, by those with whom he worked in the drafting of league legislation and policy.

Mugs was content to remain out of the limelight. Instead he worked quietly and efficiently for all of his life in the best interests of the Chicago Bears and the National Football League. For Mugs those interests worked hand in glove. Mugs was a simple man; therefore it is fitting and proper that this be a simple resolution by the board of directors of the Chicago Bears Football Club. We eagerly acknowledge our great debt to Mugs Halas; our sorrow at his death; our love for him; and our resolve to always remember all that he did on behalf of the Chicago Bears Football Club.

Appendix H
DOUG ATKINS'
INDUCTION TO THE
PRO FOOTBALL HALL OF FAME

On August 7, 1982, my father presented Doug Atkins for induction into the Pro Football Hall of Fame:

Doug Atkins was a great football player. Anyone who ever played with him, anyone who played against him, anyone who ever coached him, and anyone who ever saw him play will attest to the truth of that statement.

Doug played his college football at the University of Tennessee. Actually, he went there on a basketball scholarship but when the head football coach, General Bob Neyland, saw him playing basketball, he marveled at Doug's agility and size and soon persuaded him to play football for the Volunteers. In his senior year he was an All-American tackle. The Cleveland Browns thought enough of him to make him their first pick in the 1953 draft.

George Halas said that one of his finest trades was when he acquired Doug Atkins in 1955. The stories about Doug and his practice routines are numerous and funny. Doug believed that football should be played on Sunday afternoon. He didn't like to practice. Throughout his career with the Bears, he played with the characteristic zest of a rookie. He was awesome, and for a man his size he had great speed. His ability to leap over opposing linemen poised to block him from quarterbacks was an important factor in winning All-NFL honors in 1960, 1961, and 1963. Doug played in eight Pro Bowl games.

Doug was a Sunday football player, but he was not above a little fun even on Sunday. During the '50s, two of Doug's great buddies were Fred Williams and Bill George. When the Bears traveled for road games, they took with them one dozen footballs in a canvas sack. Coach Halas noticed that we were losing a lot of balls on the road trips, so he appointed Bill George in charge of the ball-retrieving teams and Fred Williams as the assistant. If we finished the season with the same number of balls as we started that year, each was to get $100, and for every extra ball there would be a $5 bonus. The Bears never came home with less than 12 balls and usually with 13 or 14. I can tell you how we got one extra ball on every road game.

As you know, the adrenalin is pretty high just before the kickoff. Bill George was our captain and he would go out to meet the opposing captain and the officials for the coin toss. The referee always carried a football to this little ceremony.

No matter who won the toss, Bill George would say to the referee, "Mr. Referee, I'm the captain—may I have the ball please." Invariably the referee would hand Bill the ball and he would trot to the Bear bench and hand it to Doug. If the referee or anyone else suggested he surrender the ball, he would clamp both hands on it and say, "Our captain, Bill George, told me to handle this ball." Eventually the official would shrug, go to the home-team bench, and get another ball to start the game. I don't know if Doug ever shared in the bonus money, but if he didn't, I'm sure he will want to talk to Bill George and Fred Williams.

Because of my proximity to all things involving the Bears, my heroes were always Bears, and Doug was certainly one of them. I remember one time standing next to the great Clark Shaughnessy during a practice session at St. Joseph's College at Rensselaer, Indiana. He said to me, "Now, I'll show you who the great athletes are." He blew his whistle and told the defensive squad to use a football and play volleyball utilizing the goal post. As we stood there watching these giants batting the football back and forth, Clark said to me, "The greatest athlete out there is Doug Atkins."

Doug played two years for the Cleveland Browns and 12 years for the Chicago Bears and finished his career with three years as a New Orleans Saint. Weeb Ewbank, who signed him to his first NFL contract, said of Doug, "Atkins was the most magnificent physical specimen I had ever seen."

Throughout his career Doug always felt his primary responsibility was making life miserable for opposing quarterbacks. Despite his unusual

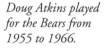

Doug Atkins played for the Bears from 1955 to 1966.

approach to practice, he always insisted that his teammates be ready by Sunday—and on Sunday, he excelled.

The stories about him are legend. As recently as last night, Doug said to me, "I don't know why they talk about these things. I don't drink; I don't smoke. Anybody's wife or sister is safe with me. I just try to get along."

For 17 years he got along in the NFL. Throughout his 12 years with the Bears, he and Coach Halas argued constantly, but they usually argued about football strategy. Usually, unfortunately for Coach Halas, Doug sometimes felt that it was important that he use the telephone to discuss matters with the coach, and all too often his timing was inopportune. He didn't hesitate to call the coach at 3:00 in the morning to tell him he didn't think a play would work.

Despite their flare-ups, they had great respect for each other, and Doug remains one Bear from that era who was never fined.

In a recent TV interview, Coach Halas was asked what he thought about Doug. We have it on tape so I know that it is true. Coach Halas said, "Doug Atkins was the greatest defensive end I ever saw."

It is a privilege and pleasure to present for induction into the Professional Football Hall of Fame, George Halas' greatest defensive end—a true football hero, Mr. Doug Atkins.